cover

inside front cover

Passion on a Plate

Passion ♥

That's what it's all about for Angela McKeller. She encourages everyone she knows to create, inspire and cultivate passion within themselves and for others – through the joy of cooking. As a caterer, a cooking instructor and award-winning recipe writer, Angela has experienced first hand how delicious food brings people together, be it old friends or new acquaintances! Whether you're new to the kitchen or have years of experience, this cookbook is for you! Angela shares with you her knowledge of *great, affordable and easy to prepare* recipes that can bring passion and joy into your life like nothing else you've experienced.

Whether it be the Fiesta Bean Dip that your colleagues at the office party can't stop discussing the next week at work, the Mediterranean Eggs Benedict that your significant other is bragging to everyone about or the delicious pound cake that was so simple to prepare that you still can't believe you made it, this cookbook has got you covered! Cooking has never been so much fun, so simple *AND* so tasty – ALL AT THE SAME TIME! Everything is explained in easy, short and concise steps with tips in every recipe so that anyone can do it!

Let the hundreds of years of experience from which Angela draws her knowledge be your guide and together, you can really give everyone something to talk about!

Passion on a Plate
Affordable and EASY Gourmet

Angela McKeller

photographs by **Erin Connolly**
additional photography by **Dan Pelch**
gadget illustrations by **Michelle LaBranche**
book design and additional illustrations by **Mary Hester**

Food styling by Erin Connolly and Angela McKeller
Graphic design by Mary Hester/2nd Floor Design
Cover photo of Angela McKeller and Leif Anderson by Erin Connolly on
location at *The Chef's Garden*, a sister company of Jake's Ice Creams &
Sorbets at 660 Irwin Street, Atlanta, GA 30312

ISBN 978-1-44956-757-6

Printed in the United States of America

Acknowledgments . . . .

There are so many names missing from the cover of this cookbook, though this work could not have been done without them. I am grateful to everyone on this list and many, many more...

Mom Buck, my great-grandmother, is my mentor and has consistently been a source of unconditional love and support since I was a very young girl. She is an incredible gift to me and the impact she has had on my life is priceless. Without her training and friendship, this cookbook would never have been possible.

I am indebted to my **husband, Michael**, for his unwavering support and for encouraging me daily to be the best that I can be for myself and for others. He has believed in my dream as strongly as I have from day 1 and because of that, you are holding this cookbook in your hands today.

To **my family**: Unconditional love and support, no matter what. I am so fortunate to have you as my family. Enough said.

To my best friend, **Nancy Smith**: Thank you for always believing in me and for being more like my sister and not just a friend.

To **Jean and Jerry Smith**: Thank you for giving me the gift of believing in myself.

To **Pat and Eric Hensley**: Thank you for showing me the importance of vision combined with follow through. Without having worked for you as a teenager, I may never have known what was possible for me.

To **Peggy Rometo**: Thank you for giving me hope. Your family is so inspiring.

To **Wendy Coughlin, PhD., and Suzi Marsh, LCSW**: I am so blessed for having had the opportunity to have worked with both of you.

To **Glenn Carver**: Thank you for your support, coaching and perspective, from the very beginning! We are very fortunate to be such great friends with "The Ambassador of Attitude"!!

To **Ralph Walker**: I so appreciate the impact that you have had on my life. Thank you so much for being such a great friend.

To **Trisha Malin**: Thank you for seeing my potential and helping me turn it into amazing things.

To **Eric and Kristi Cobb**: Thank you for so much more than I can list here, but especially my website!!

To **Roy Hinshaw**: Thank you for your assistance with this cookbook. Your generosity in lending a hand with this project made a tremendous difference and for that, I am so very grateful.

To **Dr. Elizabeth Caughey and Angelica Arueda**: For all of the laughs that have evolved into my lovely smile!

To **Erin Connolly**: Thank you for taking such ownership of this project and for helping me turn it into a GREAT cookbook! You're a great photographer, but also a great friend!

To **Michelle LaBranche**: You are such a kind soul and your illustrations add so much depth to this book. Thank you!

To **Mary Hester**: A HUGE THANK YOU TO YOU. Such a heart of gold and, again, another of many folks that really went above and beyond the call of duty. My vision was brought to life in a way I never could've imagined thanks to you!

THERE ARE MANY MORE, BUT TO EVERYONE THAT HAS HAD AN IMPACT ON MY LIFE IN ANY WAY – THANK YOU, THANK YOU, THANK YOU!

~ Angela McKeller

Table of Contents

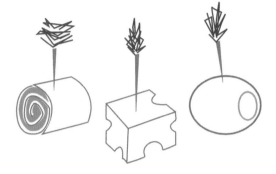

Hey!

If you are at all unsure of how to use any gadget listed in this cookbook, please be sure to ask an expert in your area. Mom Buck always told me to put safety first!

Acknowledgments...7
Preface...10-11

Munchies..12-13
Angela's Deviled Eggs 15
Fiesta Black Bean Dip 17
Best Crab Dip Ever 19
Mini-Pizzas..21

Rise and Shine..22-23
Amaretto Banana Waffles 25
Cinnamon Raisin Stuffed French
Toast Casserole 27
Baked Cinnamon & Sugar Amaretto
French Toast...29
Mediterranean Eggs Benedict 31
Mediterranean Breakfast Potatoes.............33
Spinach & Artichoke Eggs Benedict............35
Rosemary & Garlic Breakfast Potatoes.......37

Chicken..38-39
Angela's Guilt-Free Chicken Salad.............41
Stuffed Pepperoni Chicken with Pasta........43
Cheesy Spinach, Chicken and
Tomato Pie 45
Mediterranean Stuffed Chicken with
Roasted Vegetables...................................47
Delicious Fruit & Mixed Greens Salad with
Apricot Glazed Chicken 49
Thai Masaman Chicken 51
Jasmine Rice...52

Angela's Not-So-Fable About the Table #1......53

Pork..54-55

Spinach and Feta Pork
Tenderloin en Croute.............................57
Mom Buck's Pantry Soup 59
Sweet Corn Muffins 59
Peach Glazed Pork Chops.......................61
Allspice Mashed Potatoes 62
Sweet & Spiced Green Beans 63
Allspice Pork Chops with Sweet & Sour
Cherry Sauce 65
Jazzy Steamed Broccoli 66

Angela's Not-So-Fable About the Table #2......67

Seafood...68-69

Festive Fruity Field Greens Salad with
Chipotle Chile Shrimp… 71
Thai Noodle Bowl with Shrimp......................73
Spicy Tilapia with Fruit Salsa 75
Grilled Zucchini Skewers with
Orange Chipotle Marinade........................76
Citrus Rice Pilaf 77
Southwestern Chimichurri Trout 79
Hot Black Bean & Corn Salsa 80

Angela's Not-So-Fable About the Table #3......81

Beef..82-83

Angela's Beef Stroganoff...........................85
Asian Pot Roast with Asparagus &
Roasted Potatoes....................................87
Angela's Ropa Vieja................................89
Mediterranean Stuffed Bell Peppers........91
Mediterranean Rice Pilaf 92

Angela's Not-So-Fable About the Table #4......93

Italian Stuffed Zucchini Gondolas 95
Bruschetta Pasta 96

Angela's Not-So-Fable About the Table #5......97

Desserts 98-99

Brandied Peaches 101
Chocolate Hazelnut Lava Cake 103
Lemon Poppy Seed Pound Cake 105
Angela's Moist & Buttery Pound Cake 107
Strawberry Shortcake 109

Index..110-118
Healthy Substitutions 120-121
Equivalents 122
Tips for Grocery Shopping 123
Glossary 124-125

To my extraordinary great-grandmother,
Mom Buck:

Thank you for always being my friend, a great example
of how determination pays off and for all of the
Thursdays that were the highlight of my upbringing.
I dedicate this book to you.

I love you!

Preface

Cooking has long been a passion of mine, largely due to the influence of my Great Grandmother, Mom Buck. Every Thursday, Mom Buck would spend the day with our family and it was the highlight of my week for 18 years! At age 93, today she is still more than just family to me, but also a great friend and mentor. I count myself to be very blessed to be her great-grand daughter. I still call her for recipes and shortcuts!

Mom Buck taught me to throw caution to the wind! The kitchen was where we escaped reality. As early as age 3, all-purpose flour became my fairy dust. Biscuit dough became my potter's clay. Recipes were rarely used and, as a result, new concoctions and discoveries were made weekly. It was truly magical!

By the age of 12, I was hosting dinner parties. Friends of my parents would arrive to an array of foods that were a little too soupy, a little too cold or muffins that were a little too tough! Despite that, they all raved at how talented a chef I had become! With the encouragement received at each meal, my "attempts" quickly evolved into nothing short of magic and I began to feel as talented as Mom Buck!

As a teenager, Thanksgiving banquets and helping prepare hors d'Oeurves for catered events had become easy tasks for me. After seeing the how people always lingered in the kitchen during holidays or how people were always chatting around the buffet line at a big event, it didn't take long for me to figure out that food isn't just about satisfying hunger. It is a way to bring the people you love together! It was then that I realized that my passion for cooking had become much more than that. It had become a passion for entertaining, for giving of myself to others and for bringing people together. Cooking was my way of crafting **PASSION ON A PLATE!**

By the time I reached adulthood, I discovered that there weren't many cookbooks available for those of us on a budget and the easy recipes I'd found had a tendency to be bland or VERY time consuming. So, at the age of 18, I began creating my own recipes, independent of Mom Buck's assistance. I discovered how basic kitchen gadgets simplified my life, how to make exotic dishes by building on the ingredients already found in my pantry and my classmates from college began coming to my house for "home cooked meals!"

I firmly believe that bringing happiness into your life through the joy of cooking should be available to EVERYONE, not just people that have access to gourmet food markets, big bank accounts or fancy cooking classes! It was then that I began to search for just such a cookbook. A cookbook filled with tasty, exotic recipes that were affordable and EASY.

I searched high and low for a cookbook such as this. It was important to me that there be an index of ingredients by recipe so that I could look up the recipes by what was already in my pantry. Additionally, I wanted an explanation of kitchen gadgets that I may or may not have discovered. Further, I wanted a cookbook that wasn't just about meat and potatoes, just about a specific ethnic food or just about desserts. I wanted a cookbook that was a little bit of everything for any occasion! Was I being too picky? It seemed so, because locating a cookbook with such specific criteria proved to be quite a daunting task! So, instead of trying to find that cookbook, I created it!

"PASSION ON A PLATE: Affordable and EASY Gourmet" is a clear reflection of who I am. A kooky, whimsical and simple girl-next-door that loves to bring people together with simple, affordable AND tasty concoctions that will satisfy even the pickiest of eaters! From my kitchen to yours; crafting your own passion on a plate is now just pages away!

Munchies & Snacks

"Everything I eat has been
proved by some doctor or
other to be a deadly poison
and everything I don't eat has
been proved to be
indispensable for life.
But I go marching on."

George Bernard Shaw

Some words from Angela:

I have great respect for doctors and always try very hard to follow their advice. However, I must admit that it's often easier to follow the advice of my growling stomach!

Being the subject of gossip around the office is no fun, unless the gossip of the week is how you are an amazing cook following one of those bring-a-dish holiday parties!

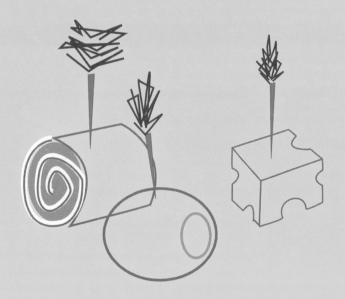

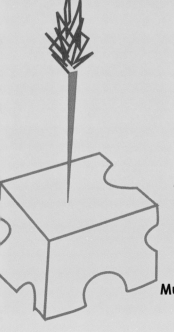

Some **Munchies** To Get That Party Going!

Angela's Deviled Eggs...15
Fiesta Black Bean Dip 17
Best Crab Dip Ever 19
Mini-Pizzas (great for kids) 21

Angela's Deviled Eggs

Angela's Deviled Eggs

6 – 12 servings

6 **eggs**
3 T. **light mayo**
1/2 tsp. **chipotle chile powder**
2 heaping T. **sweet relish**
1/4 tsp. **salt**
freshly ground pepper to taste
1/4 C. **white distilled vinegar**
(optional)

• Place 6 eggs in 2 quarts cold water (add 1 T. salt to cold water) and bring to a rolling boil.
• As soon as eggs begin to boil, turn off the eye, cover tightly with a lid and time for 10 minutes.
• Prepare an ice bath (large bowl full of ice and cover ice with cold water).
• Add ¼ c. white vinegar to ice bath so that the shells will come off easily(optional).
• When timer signals, drain water and crack all of the eggs in the pot.
• Immediately transfer cracked eggs to ice bath and time for 10 minutes.
• Peel eggs and rinse well to eliminate any egg shells.
• Cut eggs in half, length-wise, careful not to damage the whites.
• Carefully remove yolks from egg whites so as not to tear the egg whites and place yolks in medium bowl.
• Add mayo, chile powder, sweet relish, salt and pepper.
• Mix well until all lumps are gone.
• Using cookie scoop, place a small scoop of the filling in each egg white.
• Garnish with just a pinch of chipotle chile powder on each egg (Careful! A little bit goes a long way!).

Enjoy!

Notes

Tip: Cookie Scoop
Creates attractive, perfect scoops for your deviled eggs. A multitude of uses, it's a must-have in your kitchen!

Fiesta Black Bean Dip

Fiesta Black Bean Dip

6 – 12 servings

2 – 8 oz. cans of **black beans**, drained
½ c. chopped **red onion** (reserve 1 tsp)
¼ c. **sour cream**
1 tsp. **cumin**
½ tsp. minced **garlic**
1/2 c. chopped **fresh cilantro**
1 diced **avocado**
1 tsp. chopped **tomato**
2 **serrano chiles**, finely chopped (reserve a few pieces)

- In blender, combine 1st 6 ingredients.
- Pulse until you reach the smooth consistency of a dip.
- Transfer to a festive bowl and garnish with a small dollop of sour cream (use a cookie scoop) and top with reserved chopped red onion, chopped tomatoes, diced avocado and chiles.
- Insert sprig of cilantro into center of garnish.
- Serve with tortilla chips or sliced pita bread.
- Refrigerate if not serving immediately.

Enjoy!

Notes

Blender
Not just for mixed drinks and shakes!
Great for preparing dips and sauces.

Best Crab Dip Ever!

Best Crab Dip Ever!

6-12 servings

1/4 cup **sour cream**
1 (3 ounce) package **cream cheese**, softened
¼ c. **heavy cream**
½ c. **mozzarella cheese**
1 small **yellow onion**, chopped
1 tablespoon **mayonnaise**
¼ tsp **lemon juice**
¼ tsp **Worcestershire sauce**
½ tsp minced **fresh parsley**
¼ tsp minced **garlic**
1 tsp **onion powder**
1 T. **hot sauce**
6 oz. **fresh lump crab meat**

• Chop crab meat and remove shells, if needed (imitation crab may be substituted).
• In a saucepan, combine the first 12 ingredients.
• Cook over medium-low heat and stir constantly with ball whisk until the mixture is smooth.
• Add the crab and heat through (1-2 minutes).
• Serve with toast points, warm French bread or pita bread.

Enjoy!

Notes

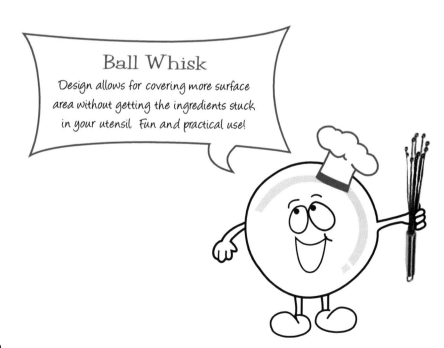

Ball Whisk

Design allows for covering more surface area without getting the ingredients stuck in your utensil. Fun and practical use!

Mini-Pizzas for Kids!

Mini-Pizzas for Kids!

8-12 servings

2 cans of **buttermilk biscuits**
(buttermilk, not the flaky kind)
1 small jar **pizza sauce**
3 c. **mozzarella cheese**

Optional toppings:
Pepperoni
Black olives
Banana peppers
Diced onions
Cubed ham
Pineapple
Bell pepper

Preheat oven to 350 degrees.
• Take 16 biscuits and press into round "pizza dough" – about 1/8" thick.

 Do not change the size of the biscuits, ie: cut them in half, or this will alter the bake time!

• Spread 2 tsp pizza sauce on each biscuit.
• Top with shredded mozzarella cheese (as little or much as you like).
• Top with any of the optional toppings (pepperoni does better on these small pizzas if you layer it before adding the cheese!).
• Bake for 15-18 minutes or until edges are lightly browned.

Enjoy!

Notes

Large Turner Spatula

Often seen slotted, like a slotted spoon, these long spatulas have many uses, but I use this spatula to remove 2 pizzas at once and the 5 minutes it saves me is a LOT of time when I have little ones constantly asking, "Is it ready yet?!"

Rise and Shine

O, with what freshness,
what solemnity and beauty,
is each new day born;
as if to say to insensate man,
'Behold! thou hast one more chance!
Strive for immortal glory!'

Harriet Beecher Stowe

Some words from Angela:

"Starting each day off with a delicious breakfast sends the message to your family that you love them and want to help them get their day off to a great start!

For a significant other that has worked hard all week, nothing says "I love you" quite like breakfast in bed!"

What's for **Breakfast**?!

Amaretto Banana Waffles 25
Cinnamon Raisin Stuffed French Toast Casserole 27
Baked Cinnamon & Sugar Amaretto French Toast 29
Mediterranean Eggs Benedict 31
Mediterranean Hollandaise Sauce 32
Mediterranean Breakfast Potatoes 33
Spinach & Artichoke Eggs Benedict 35
Spicy Hollandaise Sauce 36
Rosemary & Garlic Breakfast Potatoes 37

Amaretto Banana Waffles

Amaretto Banana Waffles

6-10 servings

3 c. all purpose **flour**
½ T. **salt**
2 T. **baking powder**
2 very ripe b**ananas**, mashed
1 T. **cinnamon**
2/3 c. granulated **sugar**
4 **eggs**
2 T. **Amaretto**
3 ½ c. **milk**
½ c. **applesauce**
Sliced **bananas** and slivered
almonds for garnish

Preheat waffle iron.
• In a large bowl, combine dry ingredients and set aside.
• In a separate bowl, combine the eggs, milk, mashed banana, amaretto and applesauce.
• Add the dry ingredients to the wet and mix only until you no longer see any dry ingredients.
• Spray waffle iron with non-stick spray.

 Spray waffle iron with non-stick spray **just** before pouring batter or the spray may burn, discolor your waffles and leave an artificial or burned taste!

• Use the amount of batter (1/2 – 1 c. batter) that suits your waffle iron and cook according to waffle iron directions (usually 3 – 5 minutes).
• Top with sliced bananas and slivered almonds.
• Serve with your favorite maple syrup.

Enjoy!

Notes

Tip | Batter Dispenser
Make beautiful pancakes and waffles without the mess! Look for a dispenser that has an airtight seal so that you can store any unused batter in the refrigerator after use.

Cinnamon Raisin Stuffed French Toast Casserole

Cinnamon Raisin Stuffed French Toast Casserole

serves 6-8

8 **eggs**
1 tsp. **vanilla**
1/3 c. **half and half**
1 loaf of **cinnamon raisin bread**, cut into cubes
3 oz. **cream cheese**, cut into small pieces
12 tsp. **blackberry jam** (or your favorite flavor jam)
Maple syrup

Preheat oven to 350 degrees.
• Spray a 9" x 9" square pan with non-stick spray.
• Place one layer of bread cubes in pan.
• Randomly place half of the cream cheese and 6 tsp blackberry jam on top of the bread.
• Add another layer of bread.
• Randomly place remaining cream cheese and blackberry jam over the bread.
• Add remaining bread to the top.
• Mix eggs, half and half and vanilla.
• Pour over the bread evenly.
• Bake for 25 – 35 minutes, or until lightly browned and springs back to the touch.
• Scoop out with a spoon or serve in squares and top with warm maple syrup.

Enjoy!

Notes

Tip Cookie Scoop

A great way to place the jam within the casserole without making a mess. Fill it about half full and voila! Fast and easy!

Baked Cinnamon and Sugar Amaretto French Toast

Baked Cinnamon and Sugar Amaretto French Toast

4 servings

8 **eggs**, beaten
1/4 c. **half and half**
2 T. **amaretto**
2 T. **korintje cinnamon**
½ c. **sugar**
4 tsp. **slivered almonds**
12 slices of **Challah bread** (cut 1" thick)

Preheat oven to 350 degrees.
• Whisk together eggs, half and half & amaretto in a bowl large enough to dip slices of bread.
• Mix sugar and cinnamon in another bowl large enough to dredge the slices of bread.
• Dip each side of bread into egg mixture and dredge in cinnamon/sugar.
• Repeat last step, dipping in egg and dredging in cinnamon/sugar again.
• Spray aluminum baking pans with non-stick spray and place french toast in baking pans.
• Bake in oven for 20 minutes.
• Flip with tongs.
• Time for an additional 10 minutes (or until both sides are nicely browned).
• Sprinkle each 3 slice serving with 1 tsp slivered almonds.
• Serve with honey or maple syrup.

Enjoy!

Notes

Tip Tongs

More control for fewer accidents! Great tool when browning in oil over high heat, when turning items during baking or when transferring hot vegetables from one dish to another.

Mediterranean Eggs Benedict with
Mediterranean Breakfast Potatoes

Mediterranean Eggs Benedict

6 servings

8 oz. **Frozen chopped spinach**, thawed, drained and patted dry with a paper towel

8 oz. softened **cream cheese**

1/2 c. **feta**, crumbled

1/4 tsp. minced **garlic**

1/4 c. **onions** (sautéed until translucent in ¼ tsp. olive oil, if desired), chopped

3/4 c. shredded **mozzarella cheese**

3 T. + 1/2 tsp. **Greek Seasoning**

4 large, ripe **tomatoes**, thickly sliced

12 **eggs**, poached

1/2 c. **plain bread crumbs**

1/2 c. finely grated **parmesan cheese**

2 **eggs**, beaten

2 T. **olive oil** (add more as needed after each tomato is done)

Preheat oven to 350 degrees.
- Combine spinach, feta, mozzarella cheese, onion, cream cheese and 3 T. Greek Seasoning in a medium bowl.
- Transfer to a small baking dish that has been sprayed with nonstick spray and bake for 10-15 minutes (or until cheeses are melted).
- Turn oven down to 200 degrees when done to keep warm.
- Mix bread crumbs, parmesan cheese and 1/2 tsp Greek seasoning.

To make breaded tomatoes:
- Coat slices of tomato in egg, dredge in bread crumb mixture and repeat previous steps.
- Heat oil in large saucepan over **medium** heat. Test your oil with a few bread crumbs to be sure the oil is hot (it should bubble around the bread crumbs). Oil should also move around in skillet like water when ready.
- Sauté tomatoes on each side until browned (about 1-2 minutes on each side) over medium heat. Any higher heat and they will burn.
- Place tomatoes in a 200 degree oven until ready to serve.

Continued on page 32

Notes

Tip

Egg Poacher

Not just for poaching eggs! Spray the cups with non-stick spray, throw in your favorite dried fruits (raisins, dried apricots, dried cranberries, etc) with 1 tsp of honey per "egg" cup and sprinkle with Ceylon Cinnamon. Time for 4 minutes or until tender! A delicious, healthy and easy dessert!

Hollandaise Sauce:

12 **egg yolks** (use an egg separator and reserve egg whites for use at a later time)

4 T. **butter**

Juice of **3 lemons** (microwave lemon for 10 seconds)

1/2 tsp. **Greek seasoning** (or as much as desired)

Notes

Tip Ice Cream Scoop

Not just for serving up dessert. Makes for a perfect portion of spread without a mess.

Hollandaise Sauce:

• In a double boiler, bring water to a steady boil over high heat then reduce heat so that water is lightly or softly boiling over a medium heat.
• Add butter, lemon and Greek seasoning and stir well until butter is melted.
• Add egg yolks, one at a time, beating quickly until butter and yolks are well blended.
• When Hollandaise is heated through, sauce is complete. Turn down heat on double boiler to a simmer and stir occasionally until ready to serve.
• If sauce becomes too thick, remove from heat, add additional 1 tsp. of butter and 1 tsp. of lemon juice occasionally.

Tips for Poaching Eggs:

• Bring water to a boil in an egg poacher.
• Spray each cup in egg poacher with non-stick spray.
• Place 4 eggs in a 4 cup egg poacher and cover with lid.
• Steam/poach for 4 minutes.
• Immediately remove tray of eggs from steaming poacher to prevent eggs from becoming overcooked.
• While poaching eggs, place 2 sautéed tomatoes on each serving plate.
• Using an ice cream scoop, scoop up 1 scoop of Greek Spinach and Cheese spread for each tomato.
• Carefully place a poached egg on top of Greek Spread.
• Top each egg with 1 - 2 T. Hollandaise Sauce.
• Garnish with a dash of Greek Seasoning.

Enjoy!

 Remember Raw or undercooked foods such as eggs can cause illness. Be sure the eggs are fresh and remember that pregnant women or women that are nursing should not consume undercooked foods for any reason.

Mediterranean Breakfast Potatoes

6 – 8 servings

1 - 5 lb. bag **red skinned potatoes**; well rinsed and cubed with skin on
Zipper baggie
2 - 3 T. **olive oil** (enough to coat potatoes)
3 T. **Greek Seasoning**
1 tsp. minced **garlic**
1 **sweet yellow onion**; finely chopped

Preheat oven to 400 degrees.
• Place all of the ingredients in the baggie with the potatoes.
• Shake VERY well to coat potatoes with the other ingredients.
• Place on large cookie sheet sprayed with cooking spray.
• Do not layer or pile the potatoes. Have one even layer.
• Bake for 45 minutes or until brown and crispy on the outside and tender on the inside.

Enjoy!

Notes

Kitchen torch

Tip Not just for Crème brûlée! Breakfast Potatoes not quite crispy enough? Casseroles not quite browned enough? Use the torch for a few seconds for finishing touches that make your meal just a bit more special

Spinach and Artichoke Eggs Benedict with
Rosemary and Garlic Breakfast Potatoes

Spinach and Artichoke Eggs Benedict

8 servings

This recipe won first place in a recipe contest sponsored by The Blake House Inn Bed and Breakfast in Asheville, NC!

1 8 oz pkg **frozen, chopped spinach**; thawed and well drained

1 – 12.5 oz. can quartered **artichoke hearts** in water; drained and chopped

1/2 T. minced **garlic**

2 cups **mozzarella cheese**, grated

1 cup **parmesan cheese**, grated

1 c. **sour cream**

1/8 c. **mayo**

16 **poached eggs** (see description of egg poacher for how)

8 large **croissants**; halved and toasted

Preheat oven to 350 degrees.

• Combine first 7 ingredients in a medium bowl.

• Transfer to a baking dish that has been sprayed with non-stick spray.

• Bake until completely melted into the consistency of a dip (approx. 25 min.).

• Lightly toast croissants (broil in oven for 1-3 minutes).

• Spread each half of croissant with a heaping tablespoon of spread.

• Poach eggs in an egg poacher by bringing a quart of water to a boil, spray the egg cups with nonstick spray, place the eggs in the tray and cover for 4 minutes.

• After 4 minutes, remove tray from poaching pan so that the eggs will not be overcooked.

• Top each croissant half with a poached egg and top with 2 T Spicy Hollandaise sauce (recipe on page 36) that was made while dip was baking.

Continued on page 36

Notes

Spinach Dip for this entree can be served with chips as an appetizer!

Tip

Egg Poacher

Not just for poaching eggs! Spray the cups with non-stick spray; add three ounces of salmon, some dill and a teaspoon of lemon juice per egg cup. Spread herb cream cheese on a bagel (or half a bagel) and serve. Healthy and tasty in just 4-6 minutes!

Spinach and Artichoke Eggs Benedict (Continued from page 35)

8 servings

Spicy Hollandaise Sauce:
12 **egg yolks**
4 T. **butter**
2 **lemons**
2 tsp. **hot sauce**
dash of **hot sauce**

Notes

Tip Ice Cream Scoop
Not just for serving up dessert. Makes for a perfect portion of spread without a mess.

Spicy Hollandaise Sauce:
- Separate eggs with egg separator and reserve whites for another recipe.
- Beat egg yolks together.
- Melt butter in a double boiler (water softly boiling over medium to medium-low heat) with lemon juice and 1 tsp hot sauce.
- When melted, slowly add egg yolks (equivalent of about one yolk at a time) so as not to cook the eggs.
- Stir constantly until heated through and serve 2 T over each egg.
- Top each egg with dash of hot sauce on the finished dish for visual presentation and a bit of a kick. *Enjoy!*

Tips for Poaching Eggs
- Bring water to a boil in an egg poacher.
- Spray each cup in egg poacher with non-stick spray.
- Place 4 eggs in a 4 cup egg poacher and cover with lid.
- Steam/poach for 4 minutes.
- Immediately remove tray of eggs from steaming poacher to prevent eggs from becoming overcooked.
- While poaching eggs, place 2 toasted croissants on each serving plate.
- Using an ice cream scoop, scoop up 1 scoop of Spinach and Artichoke Dip for each croissant.
- Carefully place a poached egg on top of dip.
- Top each egg with 1 - 2 T. Hollandaise Sauce and a dash of hot sauce (or the amount you desire).

Enjoy!

Remember Raw or undercooked foods such as eggs can cause illness. Be sure the eggs are fresh and remember that pregnant women or women that are nursing should not consume undercooked foods for any reason.

Rosemary and Garlic Breakfast Potatoes

6 – 8 servings

. . . .

1 5-lb. bag **red skinned potatoes**; well rinsed and cubed with skin on
Zipper baggie
2 - 3 T. **olive oil** (enough to coat potatoes)
3 T. **dried rosemary**
1 tsp. minced **garlic**
1 s**weet yellow onion**; finely chopped

Preheat oven to 400 degrees.
• Place all of the ingredients in the baggie with the potatoes.
• Shake VERY well to coat potatoes with the other ingredients.
• Place on large cookie sheet sprayed with cooking spray.
• Do not layer or pile the potatoes. Have one even layer.
• Bake for 45 minutes or until brown and crispy on the outside and tender on the inside.

Enjoy!

Notes

Kitchen torch

Tip Not just for Crème brulee! Breakfast Potatoes not quite crispy enough? Use the torch for a few seconds for finishing touches that make your meal just a bit more special Keep out of reach of children!

Not Your Ordinary Chicken Dish

Some words from Angela:

My goal with these recipes was for the phrase, "Hey, it tastes like chicken!" to be absent from everyone's mind. You'll be thinking, "Wow, that's even better than chicken, but it's chicken!"

Food really is passion served up on a plate. The recipe doesn't have to be difficult to be tasty. It doesn't have to be expensive to be meaningful. It just has to be served with a little bit of your soul.

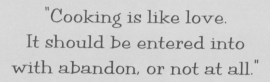

"Cooking is like love.
It should be entered into
with abandon, or not at all."

Harriet van Horne

Almost Too Good To Be Just a **Chicken** Dish!

Angela's Guilt-Free Chicken Salad 41
Stuffed Pepperoni Chicken with Spaghetti 43
Cheesy Spinach, Chicken and Tomato Pie 45
Mediterranean Stuffed Chicken with Roasted Vegetables 47
Delicious Fruit & Field Greens Salad with Apricot Glazed Chicken 49
Thai Masaman Chicken 51
Jasmine Rice 52

Angela's Guilt-Free Chicken Salad

Angela's Guilt-Free Chicken Salad

4-6 servings

1 lb. **chicken breasts**, cut into cubes and fat removed
1 ¼ c. **white seedless grapes**, cut in half or quartered
½ c. **slivered almonds**
1 c. **low-fat plain yogurt**
¼ c. **low fat mayo**
3 T. **basil**
salt and white pepper to taste
whole grain bread or crois-sants, cut in half and toasted, if desired

- Boil cubed chicken for 20 – 30 minutes or until center is no longer pink.
- Drain chicken and rinse with cool water.
- In a large bowl, mix yogurt, mayo, and basil well.
- Add chicken, almonds, and grapes. Mix well.
- Serve a heaping spoonful onto your bread of choice.
- Serve with tomato, red onion, bibb lettuce or alfalfa sprouts, if desired.

Enjoy!

Notes

Tip

Ball Whisk

The ball whisk is perfect for seeing to it that the basil stays "in" your chicken salad instead of stuck to the side of the bowl! An added bonus is that the open ends mean no grapes or almonds get stuck in your whisk!

Stuffed Pepperoni Chicken with Spaghetti

Stuffed Pepperoni Chicken with Spaghetti

4-6 servings

4 **boneless, skinless chicken breasts**, butter-flied
12 pieces **pepperoni** (or turkey pepperoni)
2 c. **mozzarella cheese**
1 – 29 oz. can **tomato sauce**
1 – 29 oz. can **crushed tomatoes**
2 oz. **tomato paste**
3 T. dried **basil**
3 T. dried **oregano**
1 T. minced **garlic**
1 T. dried **thyme** leaves
¼ c. sliced **black olives** (optional)
¼ c. Sliced **banana peppers** (optional)
½ c. Diced **onion/bell pepper** (optional)
8 oz. prepared **spaghetti**

Preheat oven to 350 degrees.
• Place butter-flied chicken breasts in greased, rectangle baking dish.
• In center of each butter-flied chicken breast, place 3 pepperoni, ¼ c. mozzarella cheese, onions and peppers (and any other "pizza toppings" you desire).
• In a medium bowl, combine tomato sauce, crushed tomatoes, tomato paste, garlic, herbs, onion and bell pepper.
• Pour tomato sauce mixture over chicken.
• Bake for 30 - 40 minutes, or until chicken is no longer pink in the center.
• Top with remaining mozzarella cheese and bake additional 10 minutes.
• While baking, prepare spaghetti.
• Serve each stuffed chicken breast with tomato sauce served over pasta.

Enjoy!

Notes

Tip

Chef's knife
Keep sharpened for fast chopping, butter-flying or cubing of meat. Many local cooking stores will offer sharpening services for FREE.

Cheesy Spinach, Chicken and Tomato Pie

Cheesy Spinach, Chicken and Tomato Pie

4-6 servings

1 **frozen pie crust**, prepared according to package directions
4 **roma tomatoes**, sliced
5 oz. **frozen chopped spinach**, thawed, drained and toweled dry
2 oz. crumbled **feta**
¼ c. chopped **yellow onion**
2 oz. **cream cheese**, softened
1 T. **Greek Seasoning**
2 **eggs**
1 c. **mozzarella cheese**
2 **boneless, skinless chicken breast**, chopped and boiled for 10 minutes

Preheat oven to 350 degrees.
• Arrange tomatoes in the bottom of the pie crust in 2 layers, reserving 2 -3 slices, discard ends of tomatoes.
• In medium bowl, combine spinach, feta, cream cheese, mozzarella cheese, Greek seasoning, eggs, mozzarella, onion and chicken.
• Mix well.
• Spread chicken and spinach filling in the pie until 2/3 full (make 2 pies if necessary).
• Top with last 3 tomato slices and bake in preheated oven for 25 – 35 minutes (until lightly golden and firm to the touch).
• Brush tomatoes with a tiny bit of water and add a dash of Greek Seasoning for garnish.

Enjoy!

Notes

Tip

Kitchen torch

Not just for crème brûlée! Great for a little extra browning on pie crust and casseroles. Keep out of reach of children!

Mediterranean Stuffed Chicken
with Roasted Vegetables

Mediterranean Stuffed Chicken with Roasted Vegetables

4-6 servings

4 **boneless, skinless chicken breasts**, butterflied

6 oz. **Frozen chopped spinach**, thawed, drained and patted dry with a paper towel

6 oz. softened **cream cheese**

1/4 c. **feta**, crumbled

1/4 tsp. minced **garlic**

2 tsp. **onions** (sautéed until translucent in 1/4 tsp. olive oil, if desired)

1/4 c. shredded **mozzarella cheese**

2 T. **Greek Seasoning**

1 small jar of **roasted red peppers**, drained and rinsed

1-20 oz. can of **quartered artichokes** in water, drained and rinsed

1 small can of **pitted black olives**, drained and rinsed

1/4 c. olive oil

Juice of 5 **lemons** (or 1/2 c. lemon juice)

Preheat oven to 350 degrees.
- Place chicken breasts in greased, rectangle baking dish.
- In a medium bowl, combine spinach, cream cheese, feta, garlic, onions and cheese and mix well.
- In center of each butter-flied chicken breast, place 2 – 3 T. of spinach mixture.
- Layer artichokes, red peppers and olives around the chicken breasts.
- In a small bowl, combine olive oil and lemon juice and pour over vegetables, around the chicken.
- Bake for 30 - 40 minutes or until no longer pink in the center, basting every 10 – 15 minutes with a silicon baster.
- Serve with rice, if desired (add 3 T. lemon juice and 2 tsp. Greek seasoning to water and then prepare rice according to package directions).

Enjoy!

Notes

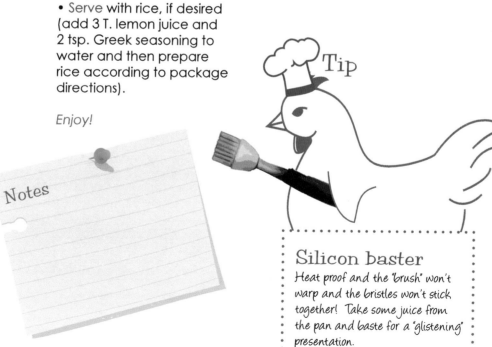

Tip

Silicon baster
Heat proof and the "brush" won't warp and the bristles won't stick together! Take some juice from the pan and baste for a "glistening" presentation.

Delicious Fruit & Field Greens Salad
with Apricot Glazed Chicken

Delicious Fruit & Field Greens Salad with Apricot Glazed Chicken

4 servings

10 oz. package of **mixed field greens**
2 large **boneless, skinless chicken breasts**
1 c. **apricot preserves**
1/8 c. **rice wine vinegar**
1 c. **dried apricots**
1 c. fresh **cherries**, pitted
½ c. crumbled **feta cheese**
½ c. **cashews**

Salad dressing:
¼ c. **granulated sugar**
1/8 c. **rice wine vinegar**
1 tsp. **Worcestershire sauce**
1/3 c. **extra virgin olive oil**

Notes

Preheat oven to 350 degrees.
• Spray a baking dish with nonstick spray and place chicken breasts in baking dish.
• Top chicken evenly with 1/2 c. apricot preserves and bake until melted.
• Mix ½ cup apricot preserves with rice wine vinegar.
• Baste each chicken breast well with apricot glaze.
• Bake for 25-30 minutes, basting again every 10 minutes until center is no longer pink.

While chicken is baking:
• Place approximately 2.5 oz. mixed field greens in each salad bowl.
• Top each salad with ¼ c. dried apricots, 1/8 c. feta, ¼ c. pitted cherries, and 1/8 c. cashews.
• Cut each chicken breast into strips horizontally.
• Serve half a chicken breast over each salad and serve your favorite rolls on the side, if desired.
• **For dressing,** mix sugar, vinegar and Worcestershire sauce very well (until sugar is dissolved).
• Add oil and shake well.

Enjoy!

Tip

Cherry Pitter
Pits cherries so the fruit remains whole for a beautiful presentation. Consider for use with olives and stuffing the centers with your favorite fillings!

Thai Masaman Chicken with Jasmine Rice

Thai Masaman Chicken

4-6 servings

5 **bay leaves**
2 cans of **coconut milk**
2-3 T. **red curry paste** (adjust amount for more or less spicy sauce)
1 tsp. ground **cardamom**
1 tsp. ground **Ceylon cinnamon**
1 tsp. ground **ginger**
1/8 c. **cashews**
2 **onions**, sliced
1 **avocado**, sliced
3 **boneless, skinless chicken breasts,** cut into strips

 Tip

Avocado Slicer
Removes avocado flesh and creates the perfect slices for topping your favorite dishes or just for a snack with chips and salsa!

 **Chicken** 51

• In a large, deep skillet, combine coconut milk, bay leaves, curry paste, • In a large, deep skillet over medium heat, combine coconut milk, bay leaves, curry paste, spices and onions over medium heat for 5 minutes.

 Add ½ tsp. of curry paste at a time and taste after each addition to be sure that the sauce is only as spicy as you would like it to be.

• Add chicken to sauce.
• Stir constantly for 15 minutes until sauce begins to thicken. Be sure to scrape the bottom of the skillet as you stir to prevent burning/sticking.
• Reduce heat and simmer and stir occasionally while preparing avocado.
• Slice avocado in half around the perimeter. Choose an avocado that feels soft like a very ripe banana.
• Using a fairly sharp knife, tap the avocado seed with the blade until it sticks into the seed.
• Twist the seed until it comes out.   Discard the pit.
• Use the avocado gadget to scoop out the flesh.

Avocado flesh darkens quickly when exposed to air. To prevent this from occurring, squeeze the juice of a lime or lemon over the avocado slices before adding to the dish.

• Serve over Jasmine Rice (recipe, pg 52) and top with 2 -3 strips of avocado per serving.

Enjoy!

Notes

Jasmine Rice

1 c. **jasmine rice**
1/8 tsp. ground **cardamom**
1/8 tsp. ground **cinnamon**
1/8 tsp. ground **ginger**
2 cups **water**

- Bring water to a boil.
- Add rice and spices.
- Immediately stir and cover pot.
- Reduce heat to simmer.
- Do not lift lid and do not stir for 20 minutes!!
- After 20 minutes, fluff rice and serve.

Enjoy!

Notes

Tip

Ice Cream Scoop
Perfect for scooping mashed potatoes or rice. To get kids excited about eating a new ethnic dish, consider making a "hill" of rice, pour sauce over it and place chicken/veggies in the "moat!"

Angela's Not-So-Fable About the Table

#1

When I was 3 years old, I would ask over and over when Thursday was coming. "Is it tomorrow? Is it tomorrow, Mommy?!" My mother must've grown tired of hearing me ask that question as though we were confined in a vehicle for a road trip asking, "Are we there yet?!". Most children that were my age looked forward to Saturday morning cartoons. Not me! I wanted it to be Thursday! Why, you ask?

Thursday was the day of the week that my FAVORITE family member would come over. My great-grandmother, MOM BUCK. She came over on holidays, too, but Thursday was her scheduled time to be with me. Yeah, yeah. I'm sure she enjoyed her visits with my mother, too, but back then, I was sure that she was actually there to see me. HA! She doted on me, loved me – one hug was never enough!

When Mom Buck would come over, the kitchen would become my playground. She was always very patient with me, giving me positive reinforcement and, most of all, she made cooking SO much fun!! I'd take a day of cooking with her over a trip to the candy shop any day of the week.

I recall my first memory of cooking with Mom Buck. I was 3 years old. We were preparing biscuits and it was SUCH a magical experience. I would watch her make a dome of flour, create a well in the middle, add the wet ingredients and mix it WITHOUT A BOWL! She was such a genius! How did she do it?! "I wanna grow up to be Mom Buck," I would think to myself.

After she mixed everything, I helped her spread out the flour over the wax paper and it was as though we were sprinkling fairy dust over the table. Then, we would pat out the dough together and it was better than play dough! I then helped her cut out the biscuits and put them on the cookie sheet. It was only a matter of time before we would be snacking on flaky, homemade buttermilk biscuits with butter and honey!

There was nothing finer that spending the day with my Mom Buck, helping in the kitchen and eating our concoctions that seemed to magically transform into the most scrumptious treats in the world! I can remember thinking in the back of my mind, "I know that today is Thursday, but can tomorrow be Thursday, too?!"

The picture above was taken of me at Mom Buck's home when I was 3 years old. The only thing better than cooking with Mom Buck on Thursdays was spending the day with her on another day at her house. As you can tell from the picture, I was happy as a lark to be there!

MORAL OF THE STORY:

Getting your child excited about the kitchen at a very early age pays dividends for both you and your little one. It builds self-esteem, creates a strong bond between the two of you and develops creativity. Besides, you just never know; your child could be the next cookbook author or celebrity chef!

Pork
a great alternative to chicken!

There is no sight
on earth more appealing
than the sight of a woman
making dinner for someone
she loves.

~ Thomas Wolfe

Some words from Angela:

Modern methods of farming means less risk associated with cooking pork. Today, pork is safe to eat when the meat thermometer reads 160 degrees F for medium all the way up to 170 degrees F for well done. This means you can focus on presentation!

I have found so much reward in simply placing a wedge of lemon alongside a Mediterranean dish, a sprig of fresh Italian parsley in the center of an Italian dish or a bowl of soup on an attractive plate accompanied by a lovely pair of muffins. Presentation is KEY. You will truly see the appreciation on the faces of everyone you love when a meal is clearly presented in a way that says "I love you."

Pork: When Chicken Just Won't Do!

Spinach and Feta Pork Tenderloin en Croute 57
Mom Buck's Pantry Soup 59
Sweet Corn Muffins 59
Peach Glazed Pork Chops....................................61
Allspice Mashed Potatoes 62
Sweet & Spiced Green Beans 63
Allspice Pork Chops with Sweet & Sour Cherry Sauce.....65
Jazzy Steamed Broccoli 66

Spinach and Feta
Pork Tenderloin en Croute

Spinach and Feta Pork Tenderloin en Croute

6-8 servings

8 oz. **cream cheese**; softened
5 oz. **frozen, chopped spinach**, thawed and drained
1 **roasted red pepper**, chopped
1/8 c. **sour cream**
3 oz. **feta cheese**
2 T. **mayonnaise**
1 T. **Greek seasoning**
1 lb. **pork tenderloin**
1 T. **garlic salt**
Pepper to taste
1 pkg. **pastry dough**
1 **egg**, beaten

Tip

Silicon Baster

Perfect for brushing egg wash onto pastry for a golden brown finish and no bristles in the dough!

Preheat oven to 350 degrees.
• Place pork tenderloin in baking dish that has been sprayed with non-stick spray.
• Sprinkle all sides with pepper and garlic salt.
• Bake for 40 minutes (or until meat thermometer registers 165 degrees).

While baking:
• In a medium bowl, mix cream cheese, sour cream, spinach, feta, red pepper, mayo & Greek Seasoning.
• Mix well with a spoon or spatula.
• In another baking dish sprayed with non-stick spray, place 1 round sheet of pastry dough on the bottom of the baking dish with the dough hanging over the sides of the pan.

After baking:
• Increase oven temperature to 450 degrees.
• When tenderloin is done, drain liquid from tenderloin and place on top of pastry dough which has already been placed in a second baking dish.
• Top tenderloin with a thick layer of spinach and cheese mixture, covering top and sides very well.
• Fold the sides of the dough over the top. It will not cover the entire tenderloin. (This is still only the 1st sheet of dough.)
• Cut a rectangle out of the 2nd round sheet of pastry dough by cutting off 2 ends and lay on top of the pork tenderloin with the edges of the round pastry underneath the rectangle.
• Fold the left and right edges on both ends inward and the bottom part upward, like wrapping a holiday gift with wrapping paper.
• Press together for a firm seal.
• Using a silicon baster or pastry brush, brush the dough with a thick layer of beaten egg.
• Bake for 15 more minutes, until pastry is a golden brown.
• Perfect for serving with a small, tossed salad!

Notes

Mom Buck's Pantry Soup
    with Sweet Corn Muffins

Mom Buck's Pantry Soup

8-12 servings

1 **ham hock** or 1 pkg.
cubed ham
2 quarts of **water**
1 pkg. **frozen mixed vegetables**
1 large can of **crushed tomatoes (24 oz.)**
½ c. **small pasta** (pastina or ditalini works well)
½ c. **rice**

- Boil ham hock in 2 quarts of water for 1 hour.
- Add frozen vegetables and crushed tomatoes.
- Bring to a boil.
- Once boiling, add rice and stir well.
- Immediately reduce heat to simmer and cover.
- Simmer for 20 minutes.
- Add pasta and cook for additional 10 – 15 minutes.
- Remove ham from bone and remove bone from soup (if using ham hock).
- When vegetables are tender, serve with sweet cornbread muffins.

Enjoy!

Sweet Corn Muffins

1/2 cup **butter**, softened
2/3 cup **granulated sugar**
1/4 cup **light corn syrup**
2 **eggs**
1/2 teaspoon **salt**
1 1/2 cups **all-purpose flour**
3/4 cup **cornmeal**
1/2 teaspoon **baking powder**
1/2 cup **milk**
2 **ears of corn**
4 c. **water**

Preheat oven to 400 degrees.
- Grease or line 12 muffin cups/liners.
- In a large bowl, cream together butter, sugar, corn syrup, eggs and salt.
- Mix in flour, cornmeal and baking powder; blend thoroughly.
- Shuck corn and remove corn silk.
- Remove corn from cob with corn zipper.
- In a small saucepan, bring water to a boil.
- Add corn and time for 2 minutes (do not wait until it returns to a boil to begin timing).
- Drain corn well.
- Add milk and corn to batter, stir well.
- Pour or spoon batter into prepared muffin cups (fill about half way).
- Bake in preheated oven for 20 to 25 minutes, or until a toothpick inserted into center of a muffin comes out clean.

Enjoy!

Notes

Tip

Corn Zipper
Makes the removal of fresh corn from the cob effortless. Much safer than using a knife!

Peach Glazed Pork Chops

Peach Glazed Pork Chops

4 servings

2 c. **peach fruit juice** (peach/grape, peach/apple – whatever you prefer)
1 can **sliced peaches**, drained
2 tsp. **pumpkin pie spice**
2 tsp. **allspice**
4 **boneless pork chops**, 1" thick
3 T. **extra virgin olive oil**
Salt and pepper

• In a small sauce pan, bring fruit juice, pumpkin pie spice and 1 tsp allspice to a boil.
• Reduce to medium for 10 minutes so that juice will reduce slightly in volume, then begin pork chops.
• In a large, deep skillet over medium heat, add extra virgin olive oil.
• Season pork chops on each side with salt and pepper to taste and ¼ tsp. allspice on each side.
• Sear pork chops for 2 minutes on each side in skillet.
• To skillet, add reduced juice, cover and time for 5 minutes.
• If juice appears to be reducing too quickly (you want to have some sauce to pour over your chops), add ¼ c. of juice as needed. Cover and time for 10 minutes, checking every 5 minutes.
• Add peaches, cover and time for 3 more minutes. Remember, add more juice if needed, ¼ c. at a time. Juice will burn if it reduces too much!
• When pork chops are no longer pink in the middle, remove from heat and serve each pork chop topped with peaches and peach glaze.

Enjoy!

Tip

Tongs
More control for fewer accidents. Great tool when browning in hot oil or when transferring the pork chops to the serving plate.

Notes

Allspice Mashed Potatoes

4 servings

12 medium to large **red-skinned potatoes**
1 T. **allspice**
1/8 c. **half and half**
3 T. **butter or margarine**
Salt and pepper to taste

• Wash potatoes with a vegetable brush and cut into quarters. They do not need to be peeled unless that is your preference.
• Remove any brown spots, if necessary.
• In a large pot, bring 6 quarts of water to a boil in a large stock pan over medium-high heat.
• Boil for 15 – 25 minutes.
• Check periodically and when potatoes are tender when pierced with a fork, drain in a collander.
• In a mixing bowl, combine potatoes, allspice, half and half, and butter.
• Mix well and serve ½ cup sized servings.

Enjoy!

Notes

Tip

Ice Cream Scoop

Perfect for scooping mashed potatoes. After scooping, use the other side to make a "well" in your potatoes for the gravy. Makes a simple, lovely presentation.

Sweet and Spiced Green Beans

4 servings

2 c. frozen **green beans**
1 tsp. **pumpkin pie spice**
1 tsp. **allspice**
1 **chicken bouillon cube**
3 ¾ c. **water**
1/4 c. **peach juice** (optional – substitute water if not using juice)

• In a medium sauce pan over medium high, bring water to a boil.
• Add bouillon cube and stir well until dissolved.
• Add green beans, spices and juice.
• Bring to a boil and boil for 5 – 10 minutes; or until beans reach your desired tenderness.
• Reduce heat to a simmer until ready to serve.

Enjoy!

Notes

Tip

Slotted Spoon

A must have in every kitchen! Keeps excess broth and sauce from mixing with other food on your plate.

Allspice Pork Chops with Sweet and Sour Cherry Sauce and Jazzy Steamed Broccoli

Allspice Pork Chops with Sweet and Sour Cherry Sauce

4 servings

2 c. **berry juice/ fruit punch**
1 c. **fresh dark, sweet cherries**, pitted
4 tsp. **allspice**
¼ c. **red wine vinegar**
1 tsp. **corn starch**
1/8 c. **water**
1 c. **vegetable or chicken broth**
4 **boneless pork chops**, 1" thick
3 T. **extra virgin olive oil**
Salt and pepper

- In a small sauce pan over med-high heat, bring fruit juice, vinegar, pitted cherries and 2 tsp. allspice to a boil.
- Reduce to medium and begin pork chops.
- In a large, deep skillet over medium heat, add extra virgin olive oil.
- Season pork chops on each side with salt and pepper to taste and ¼ tsp. allspice on each side.
- Sear pork chops for 2 minutes on each side in skillet.
- To skillet, add broth and cover for 10 – 15 minutes (or until no longer pink in the middle). Do not reduce heat.
- Check periodically to be sure broth doesn't reduce too much (add ¼ c. of water as needed if necessary) and periodically move pork chops to be sure they don't stick to the bottom.
- Dissolve cornstarch in 1/8 c. water.
- Add cornstarch mixture to juice and stir well until thickened.
- Remove from heat and transfer to a gravy boat, if you like.
- When pork chops are done, serve each pork chop with as much cherry sauce as desired.

Enjoy!

Tip

Cherry Pitter

Pits fresh cherries so the fruit remains whole for a beautiful presentation. Consider for use with olives and stuffing the centers with your favorite fillings!

Notes

Jazzy Steamed Broccoli

4 servings

. . . .

2 c. **fresh broccoli**
2 T. **butter**
1 - 2 tsp. **allspice**
4 sandwich bags - no zippers

- Place ½ cup of broccoli in each sandwich baggie.
- Dot broccoli with ½ T. butter and sprinkle evenly with ¼ - ½ tsp allspice.
- Repeat for 4 servings.
- Tie each baggie in a knot. **Do not use twist ties or baggies will catch fire!**
- Place baggies in a microwave safe bowl.
- Microwave on high for 45 seconds to 1 ½ minutes (depending on your preference of doneness).
- Using an oven mitt, remove bowl from microwave and shake each baggie so as to evenly distribute the butter and spices.
- Pull the top of the baggie, the part above the knot, toward you.
- Using the blades of your scissors, push the bottom of the bag away from you and cut so that the steam will be directed away from you.

There will be a LOT of steam which can cause SERIOUS burns, so be careful!

- Carefully empty each baggie onto each plate to serve.

Enjoy!

Notes

Baggie Shortcut

Place a serving of any veggie combo in each sandwich baggie with your favorite herbs and butter. Microwave for 1 – 2 minutes. Be careful when cutting open as the steam can cause serious burns!

Angela, age 12, with Mom Buck

Angela's Not-So-Fable About the Table

2

For years, I had been cooking and really felt as though my level of expertise FAR exceeded cake mixes and homemade chocolate chip cookies. It seemed to me, at the ripe old age of 12, that I had graduated to a greater level of expertise and I was ready to move on to dinners and dinner parties. The trick? Convincing my mother!

After many weeks of begging, she finally gave in, but insisted to know the menu before inviting anyone over. So, I told her, "Well, it's impossible to mess up breakfast. I think I'll make a really great breakfast for dinner!" She raised an eyebrow, but agreed.

So, the very next Thursday, a good friend of my mother's (easily one of the best cooks in Augusta), my great-grandmother (being another of Augusta's finest cooks) and the rest of my family gathered around the table. I had been so excited about this dinner party, but quickly my enthusiasm turned to worry. I stared at the scrambled eggs that had been sitting for at least 5 minutes, getting cold, and still the blueberry muffins were no where near done! Oh dear – I forgot about the bacon!! It was burnt and there was no salvaging it and, in my mind, it was too late to start over.

"DING" The timer sounds and my blueberry muffins are done. Thank goodness! One thing looks absolutely perfect. And I made them from scratch!! I knew that all would not be lost!

I glance at everyone's faces to see that they are all quite eager to try everything. I say a silent prayer, hoping for the best. I notice my mother's friend scooping eggs onto her plate, but the consistency didn't quite look right to me. I start to fidget. She attempts to pick up a slice of bacon, but it crumbles as she touches it. She smiles at me and in an upbeat tone of voice she says, "Looks great, Angela!" I was stunned. Could she be serious?

I start fixing my plate and grab a blueberry muffin, my favorite! I decided to cut it open to put some butter in the center, but I can hardly cut into it! OH NO! What did I do wrong?! They were like miniature bricks!

I had to put on a poker face. I couldn't let on that this meal was a disaster. I had tried too hard to convince my mother to say yes and admitting failure – I just couldn't! Besides, if I didn't notice, maybe they wouldn't either.

I look around the table and notice very quickly that my poker face worked!! Everyone began eating and RAVING over how great the food was! They must not have had any idea what I had envisioned for this dinner, because if they had pictured the dinner the way I had, they surely wouldn't like it. Since they didn't know what to expect, I suppose it was a blind spot for them!

YAY! Dinner was a success!!! But, despite how much they loved it, I was determined to figure out why the outcome hadn't matched my vision. If they thought this was great, just wait until next time!! And sure enough, the next time was INCREDIBLE!

MORAL OF THE STORY:

If you want your children to grow up excited about the kitchen and take the stress of Thanksgiving dinner off of your plate someday, never let on that their cooking is anything less than perfection!

Seafood... see it and you'll truly have to eat it!

Some words from Angela:

For years I didn't prepare fish because I thought that it was easy to mess up. I've actually learned that fish is not easy to mess up; it's actually one of the easiest things I make!

Every time I prepare a seafood lunch or dinner, people are always impressed. It has become more affordable, but is still always perceived as expensive. When dating, I would often prepare a seafood dish and it was always a big hit!

"Fish, to taste right, must swim three times - in water, in butter, and in wine."

Polish Proverb

One **Fish**, Two **Shrimp**, Three **Fish**…MORE!

Festive Fruity Field Greens Salad with Chipotle Chile Shrimp...71
Thai Noodle Bowl with Shrimp..73
Spicy Tilapia with Fruit Salsa 75
Grilled Zucchini Skewers with Orange Chipotle Marinade 76
Citrus Rice Pilaf...77
Southwestern Chimichurri Trout 79
Hot Black Bean & Corn Salsa..80

Festive Fruity Field Greens Salad
with Chipotle Chile Shrimp

Festive Fruity Field Greens Salad with Chipotle Chile Shrimp

4 servings

16 – 20 **medium shrimp**, peeled and deveined
2 T. **extra virgin olive oil**
1 tsp. **chipotle chile powder**
1/2 lb. **strawberries**, stems removed and diced
¼ **red onion**, diced
¼ c. chopped **cilantro**
1 **orange**, peeled and diced
1 c. crushed **tortilla chips**
10 oz. package of **mixed field greens**

• In 4 medium serving bowls, place 2.5 oz. of mixed field greens.
• To make salsa, combine cilantro, strawberries, oranges and red onion in a bowl.
• When dicing the oranges, reserve the juice from the oranges and add to the salsa.
• Top each salad with ¼ c. crushed tortilla chips and ¼ c. fruit salsa.
• In a large skillet over medium heat, heat 2 T. olive oil.
• In a medium bowl, toss shrimp with chipotle chili powder.
• Cook shrimp for about 2 - 3 minutes and flip half way through cooking. (So, cook 1-1½ min. on each side) They quickly become tough, so keep an eye on them!
• Shrimp are done when they are pink and no longer translucent or grey.
• Top each salad with 4-5 shrimp.

Salad Dressing:
1/2 tsp. **Dry mustard** or ¼ tsp. prepared mustard
1/8 tsp. **chipotle chile powder**
1/4 tsp. **Garlic powder**
1/2 tsp **poppy seeds**
1/4 c. **orange juice**
1/4 c. **light mayonnaise**

• Mix all ingredients well and serve as much or as little as desired.

Enjoy!

Tip

Egg slicer and wedger
Making fruit salsa for this recipe has never been easier! Lift and use both levers for dicing.

Notes

Thai Noodle Bowl with Shrimp

Thai Noodle Bowl with Shrimp

6 servings

3 packages **ramen noodles,** save seasoning packets for another purpose
2 cans **coconut milk**
2 c. **chicken or vegetable broth**
1 – 7 oz. jar pickled **baby corn**
1 c. fresh **spinach leaves**
1 c. sliced **carrots** (be sure carrots are peeled if using fresh)
1 **red onion**, cut in half and then into quarters (peel and remove ends)
1 T. **red curry paste**
1 tsp. **cinnamon**
1 tsp. **cardamom**
1 tsp. **ground ginger**
5 **bay leaves**
24-30 **medium shrimp**, peeled and deveined

• In a large saucepan over medium heat, combine coconut milk, broth, spices, red curry paste, and bay leaves.

 Add ½ tsp. of curry paste at a time and taste after each addition to be sure that the sauce is only as spicy as you would like it to be.

• Bring to a soft boil and add vegetables.
• In another saucepan, prepare ramen noodles according to package directions.
• After adding vegetables to coconut curry broth, allow liquid to come to a boil.
• Add shrimp and when liquid comes to a boil again, begin timing for 3 minutes.
• Drain noodles and add to coconut broth, veggie and shrimp mixture.
• Divide evenly into 6 bowls with each bowl getting 4-5 shrimp each.

Enjoy!

Notes

Tip

Chef's Knife
Keep sharpened for fast & easy chopping of veggies. Watch your fingers, though! Most local cooking schools offer knife skills classes & will sharpen knives for FREE!

Spicy Tilapia with Fruit Salsa,
and Grilled Zucchini Skewers

Spicy Tilapia with Fruit Salsa

4 servings

1 lb. **strawberries**, stems removed and diced
½ **red onion**, diced
½ c. chopped **cilantro**
2 **oranges**, peeled and diced
(reserve orange juice)
4 **tilapia filets**
2 tsp. **chipotle chili powder**

Preheat oven to 350 degrees.
• Season each side of tilapia filet with ¼ tsp. chipotle chile powder.
• Place in a rectangular pan sprayed with non-stick spray and Bake in preheated oven for 15 – 25 minutes, depending on thickness of tilapia filets (about 10 minutes per inch of thickness).

Tilapia should not be translucent and should flake easily when touched. Keep an eye on it after 10 minutes.

• Use a long spatula to transfer the fish to a plate so that it doesn't fall apart.
• Dice strawberries using an egg dicer and wedger.
• Lift both levers, place strawberry into holder, pull down and repeat.

Do not worry about getting the strawberries free of the wires until you get to the last strawberry.

• To make salsa, combine cilantro, strawberries, oranges and red onion in a bowl.
• When dicing the oranges, reserve the juice from the oranges and add to the salsa.
• When tilapia is done, top with 2 - 4 Tablespoons of salsa.

Enjoy!

Tip

Egg slicer and wedger
Not just for eggs! This gadget dices many different soft fruits/veggies when both levers are lifted and pressed down over your items.

Notes

Grilled Zucchini Skewers
with Orange Chipotle Marinade
4 servings

4 **zucchini**, cut into ½" - 1" thick, round pieces
1 **red onion,** cut in half and each half cut into 3 sections
4 tsp. **chipotle chile powder**
¼ c. **orange juice**
4 **wooden skewers**, soaked for 30 minutes in water to prevent burning

• If using wooden skewers, be sure to soak in water for 30 minutes before using.
• Alternate zucchini and red onion (2-3 slices thick) on each skewer.
• In an airtight container, combine orange juice and chipotle chile powder.
• Place skewers in container, cover and shake well.
• Refrigerate overnight or for at least one hour.
• Reserve marinade and place skewers on a panini press, countertop grill or outside grill over medium high heat.
• Every 2 - 3 minutes, baste with orange chipotle marinade.
• Cook for 10 – 12 minutes, or until zucchini is tender.
• Place over Citrus Rice Pilaf (recipe page 77) and baste again with orange chipotle marinade.

Enjoy!

Notes

Tip

Skewers
If wooden, be sure to soak in water for 30 minutes to prevent burning. Metal skewers come in all shapes, sizes and designs. Get creative!

Citrus Rice Pilaf

4-6 servings

· ·

1 c. **rice**
2 c. **orange juice** (pulp-free)
1 c. **water**
1 **orange**, peeled and chopped
3 T. chopped **cilantro**
1/8 c. chopped **yellow onion** (optional)

• Bring rice, water, cilantro, orange and onion to a boil.
• Add rice and stir well.
• Cover and immediately reduce heat to a simmer.
• Time rice for 20 minutes.
• Stir rice, recover and time for 10 more minutes (or until liquid is completely absorbed, if desired).
• Fluff rice and serve. If water is not completely absorbed, test doneness of rice and if it is to your liking, serve with a slotted spoon.

Enjoy!

Notes

Tip

Slotted Spoon
A must-have in every kitchen! Keeps excess broth and sauce from mixing with other food on your plate.

Southwestern Chimichurri Trout with Hot Black Bean and Corn Salsa

Southwestern Chimichurri Trout

4 servings

4 **trout filets**, ask the seafood department to remove the skin
4 tsp. **Chipotle Chile Powder**
4 c. fresh **cilantro**, chopped
1 ¼ c. **extra virgin olive oil**
2 T. minced **garlic**
Salt and Pepper to taste

Notes

Preheat oven to 350 degrees.
• Spray a baking dish with nonstick spray.
• Sprinkle each side of trout with ½ tsp. chipotle chile powder, using tongs to flip.
• Place in oven and bake for 10 minutes or until no longer translucent and flakes with a fork.

While trout is baking:
• In a blender, combine cilantro, olive oil, garlic, salt and pepper.
• Pulse to be sure cilantro doesn't get stuck in the blades.
• Periodically stop the blending and scrap sides with a spatula.
• Blend until you have the consistency of a thick pesto sauce.
• Serve 1 – 2 T. of chimichurri sauce over each trout filet.

Enjoy!

Tip

Blender
Not just for mixed drinks and shakes! Great for preparing dips and sauces.

Hot Black Bean and Corn Salsa

4 servings

2 **ears of corn**, desilked and zipped from the cob
2 cans **black beans**, rinsed and drained well
1 – 15 oz. can of **chopped tomatoes with mild green chiles**
¼ c. fresh **cilantro**, chopped

- In a saucepan over medium high heat, bring 4 cups of water to a boil.
- When water is boiling, add corn.
- Boil for four minutes and drain.
- In a separate saucepan, add black beans, chopped tomatoes and cilantro.
- Stir well and bring to a boil.
- Add corn, stir well and time for 2 minutes.
- Reduce to a simmer until ready to serve, but corn will become tough if left to simmer for too long, so serve as quickly as you can! About 4 minutes total is all the corn needs!

Enjoy!

Notes

Tip

Corn Zipper
Makes the removal of fresh corn from the cob effortless. Much safer than using a knife!

Angela's Not-So-Fable About the Table

#3

By the time I was 16 years old, I had become quite the chef. I had helped with the family catering business, was preparing casseroles for the holidays and making fancy desserts. Intimidated by a double-boiler? Are you kidding? No way!! Anyway...

I had been taught that there were some key qualities that a true Southern lady should possess. For example, always take care to keep up with appearance because you just never know who you may run into. Yes, even checking the mail was an event that required hair and makeup and, I must confess, I wasn't always up to the challenge. Second, always keep things tidy and clean. Ok. I fully admit that my bedroom had a long way to go. Third, cooking should be second nature. Yay! That one I had fully mastered! There were others, but these I remember well!

Moving on, I had briefly dated a few boys and, admittedly, it wasn't going very well for me. I was thinking that perhaps my mother had been onto something. So, I started to keep up a bit more with my appearance. Hey, that hair you see in my picture – that was no easy task! The waterfall, I frequently called it. HA! Despite what you may be thinking (and I'm thinking it, too, I can assure you), it did help me get dates to look like that, but still nothing of substance. What was I doing wrong??

After quite some time of not being able to keep a boyfriend, I figured I would skip to step three since no boyfriend of mine was going to see my bedroom with my dad being leery of letting him past the front porch. HA! I made the decision to showcase my skills and, miraculously, I landed a couple of dates with a popular football player. He'd better look out! Nothing like turning on the charm learned from Mom Buck's School of Culinary Arts!

I figured that this new recipe for a fantastic Devil's Food Cake with Seafoam Icing that I had discovered was sure to impress my new beau. The cake was so moist and the icing so light and airy that every bite would melt in your mouth! I simply could not wait to invite him over to try it. This strategy was going to work. I just knew it!

Date night arrived and he had a piece of my cake. He appeared to be quite impressed and even asked to take some with him to take to his family. It worked! Everyone knows that the way to man's heart is through his stomach! Right? Right...

Once on our way to our destination, we began discussing our hobbies and what each of us liked to do. I listed several hobbies, but really talked about how much I loved cooking. He curtly replied, "So what are you going to do when you graduate? Spend all day cooking?" At the time, I was considering being a high school teacher, but frankly, I thought that cooking all day would be ideal. Why hadn't I thought of that?! I sure didn't tell him I was thinking that, though! Then I began to think, "What if I did want to be a chef? What if I did want to make a career out of cooking?"

Needless to say, there were no more dates for the two of us in our future. Back to the drawing board!

MORAL OF THE STORY:

Never underestimate the value of cooking. Someone just might make a career out of it, write a cookbook and include a silly story about you in it!

Beef...options, options, options!

Some words from Angela:

I suppose it is a good idea to be careful of how much red meat we consume. But, we are also advised to cut back on sugar, caffeine and some even say dairy. After an entire five seconds of pondering to what extent I will practice self-discipline, I simply carry on with my pot roast for dinner and enjoy a delicious dessert served with my favorite cup of coffee with extra cream afterwards!

Self-discipline? Hmm...perhaps I'll look that up in the dictionary some time!

"Vegetables are interesting but lack a sense of purpose when unaccompanied by a good cut of meat".

Fran Lebowitz

Beef...so many possibilities!

Angela's Beef Stroganoff..85
Asian Pot Roast with Asparagus and Roasted Potatoes....87
Angela's Cuban Ropa Vieja 89
Mediterranean Stuffed Bell Peppers....................................91
Mediterranean Rice Pilaf 92
Italian Stuffed Zucchini Gondolas 95
Bruschetta Pasta 96

 Beef 83

Angela's Beef Stroganoff

Angela's Beef Stroganoff

4 servings

Slow cooker liner (optional)
½ lb. **boneless shoulder roast**
2 large **yellow onions**
1 can **cream of chicken soup**
1 can **cream of mushroom soup**
2 c. **water**
1 can **beef broth**
1 package of **white button mushrooms**, brushed clean and quartered
1 c. plain **no-fat yogurt**
2 c. prepared **egg noodles**

- Line a slow cooker with a slow cooker liner for easy clean up(optional).
- Place roast in slow cooker.
- In a medium bowl, mix soups, broth and water until well blended.
- Pour mixture over pot roast.
- Turn heat up to high and cover with lid.
- Leave to cook for 6 hours.
- Peel onion, cut off the ends and cut into 4 pieces by cutting the onion in half and then cutting each half in half again.
- Add onion and mushrooms to roast.
- Cook for additional 30 minutes.
- When done, pull roast apart with two meat forks and stir in yogurt.
- Serve each serving over ½ c. egg noodles.

Enjoy!

Notes

Tip

Tongs
Use the tongs to transfer the perfect servings of beef and veggies to your plate. Use a regular spoon for plenty of sauce!

Asian Pot Roast with Asparagus and Potatoes

Asian Pot Roast with Asparagus and Potatoes

6-8 servings

1 – 1 lb. **shoulder roast**
2 **Idaho potatoes**, sliced thickly
16 **asparagus stems**
2 **yellow onions**, quartered
¼ c. **rice wine vinegar**
¼ c. **low-sodium soy sauce**
1 c. **water**
2 tsp. **ground ginger**
2 T. minced **garlic**
2 T. **honey**

Preheat oven to 350 degrees.
• Place roast in a rectangle baking dish.
• Cut 6-8 "pockets" in the roast and fill with the minced garlic.
• Any remaining garlic, place in baking dish around the roast.
• Pour vinegar and soy sauce over roast.
• Pour water into pan (NOT over the roast).
• Dust roast with ground ginger.
• Top roast with honey. Honey doesn't have to cover the entire roast.
• Bake for 1 hour, covered with foil.
• Remove from oven and add potatoes and onion.
• Cover again and bake for an additional 50 minutes.
• Rinse asparagus in a bowl of water, changing water once.
• Snap off ½" to 1" on the "trunk" side of the asparagus.
• Remove roast from oven and add asparagus to pan.
• Cover again and bake additional 10 minutes.
• Serve immediately.

Enjoy!

Notes

Tip

Silicon Baster
Heat proof and the bristles won't warp or stick together! Take juice from the pan and baste before serving for a "glistening" presentation!

Angela's Cuban Ropa Vieja

Angela's Cuban Ropa Vieja

8-12 servings

Slow cooker liners (optional)
1 **flank steak** (1 - 1 1/4 lb.),
marbled but not too much fat
4 tsp. **garlic salt**
2 T. **extra virgin olive oil**
2 c. **water**
2 c. **beef broth**
2 - 14.5 oz. cans **crushed
tomatoes with mild green
chiles** (do not drain)
1 heaping Tablespoon of
minced **garlic**
1 c. **red wine** of your choice
(optional)
10 oz. **fajita veggies** (5 sliced
bell peppers and 1 large sliced
onion)
1 handful of **cilantro**, chopped
6 oz. **tomato paste**

- In a large skillet over medium high heat, heat 2 T. extra virgin olive oil (it will move in the pan like water).
- Season flank steak on both sides with garlic salt (2 tsp each side).
- Brown seasoned flank steak on each side, about 4 minutes each.
- Place slow cooker liner in your slow cooker (optional).
- In slow cooker, add water, beef broth, garlic, red wine & tomatoes with green chiles.
- Stir well and add flank steak (you may cut it in half if it won't fit all in one piece).
- Turn slow cooker up to high heat and let cook for 6-8 hours.
- After several hours, add cilantro and tomato paste.
- Stir until tomato paste is dissolved.
- Add fajita veggies and let cook 30 more minutes.
- Serve with your favorite side of saffron rice and enjoy!

Enjoy!

Notes

Tip

Tongs
For Ropa Vieja, use tongs to plate up the beef and veggies. This will ensure that you're getting the right serving for each plate!

Mediterranean Bell Peppers with Rice Pilaf

Mediterranean Stuffed Bell Peppers

4 servings

4 small to average sized **bell peppers**
½ lb. **extra lean ground beef**
¾ c. **crushed tomatoes**
1 **lemon**
4 T. **Greek Seasoning**
1 tsp. **garlic**
¼ **low-fat feta cheese**
1 **egg**
1 c. **plain bread crumbs**
1/8 c. **red wine vinegar**

Preheat oven to 350 degrees.
• Cut the tops off of the bell peppers, remove the stem from the center of the tops and set to the side.
• Remove seeds and white "columns" from inside of the bell peppers.
• Cut 4 small holes in the bottom of each bell pepper so that the juice from the beef stuffing will drain while baking.
• In a large bowl, combine ground beef, crushed tomatoes, juice of one lemon, Greek seasoning, garlic, feta, egg, bread crumbs and vinegar.
• Stir well.
• Stuff bell peppers with 4 oz. ground beef stuffing each (1/2 cup).
• Line a baking pan with non-stick foil for easy clean up, if desired.
• Place bell peppers and tops in baking pan and bake for 1 hour.
• Place stuffed bell peppers on a serving of Mediterranean Rice Pilaf (recipe on page 92), if desired.
• Situate the tops of the bell peppers on top of the stuffed bell peppers, if desired, and serve.

Enjoy!

Tip

Grapefruit knife
Not just for grapefruits!
The angle and dual sided blade makes removing the seeds and veins of the bell pepper much easier!

Notes

Mediterranean Rice Pilaf

4-6 servings

3 c. **water**
1 c. uncooked, **long grain rice**
¾ c. **crushed tomatoes**
1 tsp. **garlic**
2 T. **red wine vinegar**
1 **lemon**
2 tsp. **Greek seasoning**

• Combine water, crushed tomatoes, garlic, vinegar, juice of one lemon and Greek Seasoning in a saucepan.
• Bring to a boil.
• Add rice and stir well.
• Immediately reduce to simmer and cover.
• Time for 30 minutes, WITHOUT lifting the lid.
• Stir well and serve or continue to cook for additional 5 minutes until water is absorbed , stirring occasionally.
• If you do not wish to wait until all of the water is absorbed, test for doneness and serve with a slotted spoon.

Enjoy!

Tip

Slotted Spoon
A must-have in every kitchen! Keeps excess broth and sauce from mixing with other food on your plate.

Notes

Angela's Not-So-Fable About the Table

4

College was a great chapter for me. I loved my classes, my professors were outstanding and my fellow classmates were great! When I couldn't afford to buy all of my books, I had friends that would go in half on the books or they would simply let me borrow their books. We chose to study together in exchange for their generosity since I was a really good note taker in class and typically had a very good idea of what would be on the exams. I was just trying to save money, but I later found out that research has proven that people that study together, excel together. BONUS!

However, less expense for books, better study habits and better grades weren't the only upside to spending so much time with my newly found good friends! I mean, we had to eat, right? Well, I was very fortunate that my fellow classmates enjoyed my cooking so much because this turned out to be another great way for me to save money (and for them to minimize how homesick they felt)!

I must admit, I was quite shocked when my friends would regularly ask, "Hey, do you think you could cook tonight? We are SO sick of ordering pizza! If you'll cook, we'll go get the groceries! Pleeeeeaaaaseeee!!!" My friends, all of us in our early 20's, preferred my cooking to PIZZA? How could I say no to that?! Besides, I absolutely loved to cook, so I would answer, "Ok...tell me what you're in the mood for and I'll make a list for you." While they were shopping, I would organize our study materials. What a win-win situation!

Oddly enough, they usually wanted "Kuntry Kookin," something to remind them of home. We were all Southern Belles from various parts of Georgia, you know. So, we would have meatloaf that would melt in your mouth, the creamiest, homemade mashed potatoes or a piping-hot, flavorful pot roast with new potatoes and field peas.... They would just ooooh....and ahhhhh....over the food as though they'd never tasted anything so divine. They always stared in awe as I prepared an amazing dinner and once dinner was served, never had I seen a room full of girls in their early 20's become so quiet in my entire life!

Who says college students have to be stuck with 10¢ packages of noodles every night or cheap frozen pizzas for dinner? Not if you were my friend!

It was an incredibly rewarding experience to know that I could make a difference to my friends in such a way. They always believed that there was no way they would be able to duplicate my cooking, so my first thoughts about a cookbook began to culminate within my mind back in those days. My meals were tasty, affordable and easy to prepare. I would think to myself, "Everyone needs to be able to cook like this!" In the picture above, you'll see one of my best college buddies, Kippie, and myself. Still great friends years later!

MORAL OF THE STORY:

Cooking is much more than just putting a meal on the table. My cooking has always made a HUGE difference to my friends and not being afraid to cook for a group saved me quite a bit of cash during a time in which I really needed to save the money! I also established lasting friendships for life!

Italian Stuffed Zucchini Gondolas
with Bruschetta Pasta

Italian Stuffed Zucchini Gondolas

12 servings

6 medium-large **zucchinis**
1 medium **sweet yellow onion**, chopped
1 T. **extra virgin olive oil**
1 cup **tomato sauce**
¼ c. **Italian-style dried bread crumbs**
1 **egg**
1 cup shredded **mozzarella cheese**
¼ cup grated **Parmesan cheese**
2 T. **dried basil**
2 T. **dried thyme**
1 T. **oregano**
1 tsp. minced **garlic**
¼ lb. **ground beef**
6 **garlic bread sticks**

Notes

Preheat oven to 350 degrees.
• Slice each zucchini in half lengthwise.
• Hollow out the zucchini with a vegetable corer and cut zucchini in half again.
• Chop the zucchini that was scraped out into small pieces and transfer to large bowl.
• Make 2 small holes in the bottom of each zucchini "boat" so that liquid can drain as it cooks (about the size of the top of a tack).
• Place zucchini boats into baking dish sprayed with non-stick spray.
• Saute onions in skillet with olive oil over medium heat.
• When onions are translucent, transfer to a large bowl with chopped zucchini.
• Combine zucchini, bread crumbs, mozzarella cheese, ground beef, onions, basil, oregano and thyme.
• Add egg and tomato sauce.
• Mix well.
• Spoon mixture into hollowed out zucchini.
• Bake for 40 minutes.
• Remove from oven and top each zucchini boat with freshly grated parmesan cheese.
• Bake 3-5 more minutes or until cheese is melted or use a kitchen torch (3 inches away from surface) until cheese is melted.
• Spear each "gondola" with a garlic bread stick to give the appearance of an "oar." *Enjoy!*

Tip

Vegetable Corer
Great gadget for coring vegetables, fruits or removing seeds. Various uses – get creative!

Bruschetta Pasta

6 servings

• •

12 oz. **spaghetti**
1 tsp. **salt**
1 T. **extra virgin olive oil**
1 ¼ c. **tomato sauce**
3 ¼ c. (26 oz.) **chopped tomatoes**
1/8 c. **balsamic vinegar**
1 c. **red onions**
2 tsp. **dried basil**
2 tsp. **dried thyme**
2 tsp. **dried oregano**

• Bring a pot of water, 1 tsp. salt and 1 T. extra virgin olive oil to a steady boil.
• Add spaghetti and boil for 10-12 minutes.

While pasta is boiling:
• Sauté red onions in 1 T. extra virgin olive oil until translucent/light in color.
• In large saucepan, combine tomato sauce, chopped tomatoes, sautéed red onions, balsamic vinegar and herbs.
• Bring sauce to a boil.
• Drain spaghetti and add to sauce.
• Stir well.
• Reduce to simmer until ready to serve.

Enjoy!

Notes

Tip

Slotted Spoon
Some slotted spoons are designed to retrieve the pasta as well as drain excess sauce. Consider looking for one of those! Your local kitchen store should be familiar with them.

Angela's Not-So-Fable About the Table

#5

Valentine's Day was fast approaching and I didn't have a date. What's a girl to do? I was in my mid20's, had just begun my new life in corporate America and only had a handful of single friends. Hmmm...what to do, what to do.

I know! How about a singles Valentine's Day Party and with the theme being how much we love ourselves despite being able to find true love! I had 5 definites and a few maybes. It was a small dinner party, but I still had more dates than most people have on Valentine's Day. I couldn't wait!

The day before the party, I created a menu and prepped everything that could be done in advance. I was a professional now and figured that Valentine's could be a two-fold celebration – a celebration of having GREAT friends that loved me (and I them), as well as a party to celebrate my new professional career direction! Everything was done, including the Red Velvet Cake. I had designed it to be a frosty, "cold" white (cream cheese frosting) with a blood red, moist cake and a fruity filling that would ooze a fruit filling when you "broke" into it as if to break someone's heart! Hey, we were young, single, and beautiful. We were heartbreakers...weren't we?! Everyone thought it was a genius idea!

The day of the party, everyone arrived and I began offering drinks and appetizers. Everyone was so impressed and just 5 minutes into the party, we were already having a great time! The chicken dish I had prepped was going to need to cook for nearly an hour, so I preheated the oven and we continued to laugh, enjoy our wine, munch on nifty little snacks and tell stories of past loves lost.

Suddenly, I notice that there is an odor coming from the kitchen. It wasn't bad, it's just that it shouldn't smell like anything since the oven is empty and is simply preheating! I then notice that it's kind of a fruity aroma. Hmm... I excuse myself from the myriad of laughter and go check the oven to see what it could possibly be. I was completely unprepared for what I found! My bleeding heart cake was...well, bleeding!!

I had forgotten that I had run out of room in my fridge and I needed a cake taker. When I made the cake, it was less than 18 hours before my guests would be arriving, so I thought to myself, "Oh well, no time for that! I'll just store it in the oven until everyone arrives." Now, the frosting and strawberry center was running all over the place and it was a dreadful mess! Suddenly, I burst into laughter. Nothing was going to ruin my dinner party!

After hearing uncontrollable laughter coming from the kitchen, my guests hurry in to find red, gooey, fruity filling, dripping to the floor. They all started laughing hysterically and one friend said, "Yep, you said a bleeding heart cake and you weren't kidding!" They were such good sports about it and helped me clean up the mess, laughing the entire time and we made an executive decision to go out for coffee and dessert after dinner. Here, I am pictured with friends, Denise & Kippie.

We all took pictures (this being one of them) and to this day, we all have a picture of this event framed and displayed somewhere in our homes. Perfection is a lofty goal. Imperfection is priceless!

MORAL OF THE STORY:

Throw caution to the wind and invite everyone over for dinner. If something goes haywire, there is always takeout available as a plan B and a GREAT story to tell for years to come afterwards!

Sweets... for your sweetie or just for your sweet tooth!

"Vegetables are a must on a diet.
I suggest carrot cake, zucchini
bread and pumpkin pie."

Jim Davis

Some words from Angela:

Every time I tell someone I have a headache, they suggest taking one extra Ibuprofen than the bottle suggests. So, if you are suffering from a sweet tooth, doesn't it just make sense that five pieces of cake would remedy that sweet tooth much more quickly than just one?

Also, It has been said that variety is the spice of life. That is why I always suggest that people have at least 3 desserts after dinner!

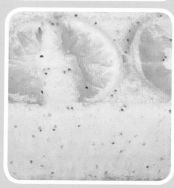

Got a **Sweet Tooth**?

Brandied Peaches...101
Chocolate Hazelnut Lava Cake.............................103
Lemon Poppy Seed Pound Cake...........................105
Angela's Moist and Buttery Pound Cake...............107
Strawberry Shortcake..109

Brandied Peaches

Brandied Peaches

4 servings

8 T. **Tupelo Honey**
2 – 15 oz. can of **sliced peaches**
4 T. **Ceylon Cinnamon**
1/2 c. **brandy**

• Combine peaches, honey, cinnamon and brandy in a medium skillet over medium-high heat.
• Boil peaches for 5-8 minutes (until alcohol evaporates; you will no longer detect the aroma of alcohol).
• Reduce for 5-10 minutes, until sauce is slightly thicker, almost a syrup.
• Reduce to simmer until ready to serve.
• Serve with a small cookie scoop of vanilla bean ice cream, if desired.

Enjoy!

If you aren't comfortable using a torch, flambé with a LONG match. Keep your distance and 30 seconds after adding brandy, ignite for an impressive demonstration!

Notes

Tip

Kitchen torch

Flambé anyone? Stand a foot away, turn your face away and ignite the brandy. Lovely! DO NOT flambé with the vent fan over the stove running!

Chocolate Hazelnut Lava Cakes

Chocolate Hazelnut Lava Cakes

8 servings

⭐ As seen prepared by Angela McKeller and Paula Deen on The Food Network Show, *Paula's Party!* ⭐

8 oz. **semi-sweet baking squares**
1 cup **butter**
2 cups **powdered sugar**
4 **eggs**
4 **egg yolks**
¾ c. **flour**
2 T. **hazelnut extract**
Hazelnut liqueur
Chocolate hazelnut spread
Vanilla ice cream
Chocolate shavings

Preheat oven to 425°F.
• Spray 8 - 4oz ramekins with non-stick spray.
• Place on baking sheet.
• Microwave chocolate and butter in large microwaveable bowl on high for 1 min. or until butter is melted.
• Stir with wire whisk until chocolate is completely melted.
• Blend in eggs and egg yolks one at a time, so that the eggs do not cook, then add hazelnut extract.
• Stir in flour and powdered sugar.
• Divide batter evenly among prepared custard cups.
• Bake 13 to 14 minutes or until sides are firm but centers are **soft**.

Note that they will NOT look done in the centers! Don't worry, it's fudge sauce!

• Let stand 1 minute.
• Carefully run a small knife around cakes to loosen.
• Invert cakes onto dessert dishes, pour ¼ tsp. hazelnut liqueur on top and spread a thin layer of chocolate hazelnut spread on top of each lava cake.
• Spread gently so as not to damage the cakes – easiest if cookie scoop is used, hazelnut spread is given a few seconds to melt and then spread with an offset mini-cake spatula.
• Serve immediately, topped with a cookie scoop size scoop of vanilla ice cream and chocolate shavings or dust with cocoa powder.

Enjoy!!

Ball whisk Tip

Design allows for covering more surface area to be sure NO chocolate is left on the sides of the bowl. Fun and practical use!

Notes

Lemon Poppy Seed Pound Cake

Lemon Poppy Seed Poundcake

8-12 servings

1 c. **unsalted butter**, softened
1/2 c. **apple sauce**
2 3/4 c. **granulated sugar**
6 **eggs**
1 T. Pure **Vanilla Extract**
3 T. **lemon extract**
2 T. **poppy seeds**
3 c. sifted **all-purpose flour**
8 oz. (1 c.) **plain yogurt**
1 **lemon**, sliced and seeds removed

Preheat oven to 350 degrees.
• Spray an aluminum (not a dark pan) angel food cake pan (9 3/4" diam., 4" high) with nonstick spray that contains flour or grease and flour the pan.
• Lie lemon slices on the bottom of the angel food cake pan (or whichever kind of pan you choose –mini-loaves make great gifts).
• Cream butter and sugar together.
• Add applesauce, eggs, vanilla extract, lemon extract and poppy seeds.
• Add flour and yogurt gradually, alternating ingredients until well blended.
• Pour cake batter into angel food cake pan over the lemon slices; pan should not be more than ¾ of the way full, no matter what type of pan is used.
• Bake for 1 hour 10 minutes or until cake springs back when touched.
• Allow to cool for 20 minutes and invert onto cooling rack for 1 hour.
• Serve on a cake server and enjoy!

Enjoy!!

Notes

Tip

Aluminum Bakeware

It is important to use light-colored pans when baking. They don't retain as much heat as dark pans, so the edges don't cook too quickly or burn!

Angela's Moist and Buttery Pound Cake

Angela's Moist and Buttery Poundcake

8-12 servings

1 c. **unsalted butter**, softened
1/2 c. **apple sauce**
2 3/4 c. **granulated sugar**
6 **eggs**
1 T. Pure **Vanilla Extract**
1 T. **butter extract**
3 c. sifted **all-purpose flour**
8 oz. (1 c.) **plain yogurt**

Preheat oven to 350 degrees.
• Spray an aluminum (not a dark pan) angel food cake pan (9 3/4" diam., 4" high) with non-stick spray that contains flour (ie: Baker's Joy) or grease and flour the pan.
• Cream butter and sugar together.
• Add applesauce, eggs, vanilla and butter extract.
• Add flour and yogurt gradually, alternating ingredients until well blended.
• Pour cake batter into angel food cake pan; pan should not be more than ¾ of the way full.
• Bake for 1 hour 10 minutes or until cake springs back when touched.
• Allow to cool for 20 minutes and invert onto a cooling rack for 1 hour.
• Carefully transfer to a cake server/cake taker.
• Dust with powdered sugar, fill center with strawberries, party favors for any occasion or serve plain.

Enjoy!!

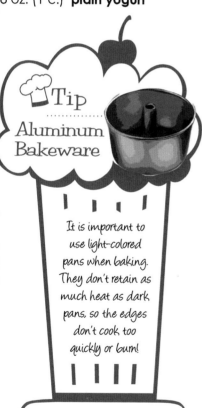

Tip

Aluminum Bakeware

It is important to use light-colored pans when baking. They don't retain as much heat as dark pans, so the edges don't cook too quickly or burn!

Notes

Strawberry Shortcake

Strawberry Shortcake

12 - 16 servings

1 lb. **strawberries**, stems removed and diced
1/8 c. **granulated sugar**
1 T. **Ceylon cinnamon**
12 – 16 slices of your **favorite pound cake** (great recipe, pg. 107)
Non-dairy whipped topping or **whipped cream**

- Combine strawberries, sugar and cinnamon in a medium sized bowl.
- Mix well.
- Cover with an airtight lid or plastic wrap.
- Refrigerate for 1 hour.
- Stir well and spoon 1 – 2 T. strawberries over each slice of pound cake.
- Top with whipped topping or whipped cream and serve.

Enjoy!!

Notes

Tip

Egg slicer and wedger

Not just for eggs! This gadget dices many different soft fruits/veggies when both levers are lifted and pressed down over your items.

Index

Allspice:
Allspice Mashed Potatoes, 62
Jazzy Steamed Broccoli, 66
Peach Glazed Pork Chops, 61
Sweet and Sour Cherry Pork Chops, 65
Sweet and Spiced Green Beans, 63

Almond(s):
Amaretto Banana Waffles, 25
Angela's Guilt-Free Chicken Salad, 41
Baked Cinnamon and Sugar Amaretto
French Toast, 29

Amaretto:
Amaretto Banana Waffles, 25
Baked Cinnamon and Sugar Amaretto
French Toast, 29

Apple Sauce:
Amaretto Banana Waffles, 25
Angela's Moist and Buttery Pound Cake, 107
Lemon Poppy Seed Pound Cake, 105

Apricot(s):
Dried:
Fruity Field Greens Salad with Apricot
Glazed Chicken, 49

Artichoke(s):
Canned:
Mediterranean Stuffed Chicken with
Roasted Vegetables, 47
Spinach and Artichoke Eggs Benedict, 35

Asparagus:
Asian Pot Roast with Asparagus and Potatoes, 87

Avocado(s):
Fiesta Black Bean Dip, 17
Thai Masaman Chicken, 51

Baking Powder:
Amaretto Banana Waffles, 25
Sweet Corn Muffins, 59

Banana Peppers:
Mini-Pizzas, 21
Pepperoni Stuffed Chicken, 43

Banana(s):
Amaretto Banana Waffles, 25

Basil:
Dried:
Angela's Guilt-Free Chicken Salad, 41
Bruschetta Pasta, 96
Italian Zucchini Gondolas, 95
Pepperoni Stuffed Chicken, 43

Bay Leaves:
Thai Masaman Chicken, 51
Thai Noodle Bowl with Chipotle Chile Shrimp, 73

Beef:
Flank Steak:
Angela's Slow Cooker Ropa Vieja, 89
Ground:
Italian Zucchini Gondolas, 95
Mediterranean Bell Peppers, 91
Shoulder Roast:
Angela's Easy Beef Stroganoff, 85
Asian Pot Roast with Asparagus
and Potatoes, 87

Bell pepper(s):
Any:
Angela's Slow Cooker Ropa Vieja, 89
Mediterranean Bell Peppers, 91
Mini-Pizzas, 21

Pepperoni Stuffed Chicken, 43
Roasted Red:
Mediterranean Stuffed Chicken with
Roasted Vegetables, 47
Spinach and Feta Pork Tenderloin en Croute, 57

Black Beans:
Fiesta Black Bean Dip, 17
Hot Black Bean and Corn Salsa, 80

Bouillon Cubes:
Chicken:
Sweet and Spiced Green Beans, 63

Brandy:
Brandied Peaches, 101

Bread:
Cinnamon Raisin:
Cinnamon Raisin Stuffed French
Toast Casserole, 27
Challah:
Baked Cinnamon and Sugar Amaretto
French Toast, 29
Croissants:
Spinach and Artichoke Eggs Benedict, 35
Crumbs:
Italian Zucchini Gondolas, 95
Mediterranean Bell Peppers, 91
Sticks:
Italian Zucchini Gondolas, 95
Wholegrain:
Angela's Guilt-Free Chicken Salad, 41

Broccoli:
Jazzy Steamed Broccoli, 66

Broth:
Beef:
Angela's Easy Beef Stroganoff, 85
Angela's Slow Cooker Ropa Vieja, 89

Chicken:
Sweet and Sour Cherry Pork Chops, 65
Thai Noodle Bowl with Shrimp, 73
Vegetable:
Sweet and Sour Cherry Pork Chops, 65
Thai Noodle Bowl with Shrimp, 73

Butter Extract:
Angela's Moist and Buttery Pound Cake, 107

Butter:
Allspice Mashed Potatoes, 62
Jazzy Steamed Broccoli, 64
Angela's Moist and Buttery Pound Cake, 107
Chocolate Hazelnut Lava Cakes, 103
Lemon Poppy Seed Pound Cake, 105
Sweet Corn Muffins, 59

Canned Buttermilk Biscuits:
Mini-Pizzas, 21

Cardamom:
Ground:
Jasmine Rice, 52
Thai Masaman Chicken, 51
Thai Noodle Bowl with Shrimp, 73

Carrots:
Thai Noodle Bowl with Shrimp, 73

Cheese:
Cream:
Best Crab Dip Ever, 19
Cheesy Chicken and Spinach Pie, 45
Cinnamon Raisin Stuffed French
Toast Casserole, 27
Mediterranean Eggs Benedict, 31
Mediterranean Stuffed Chicken with
Roasted Vegetables, 47
Spinach and Feta Pork Tenderloin
en Croute, 57

Feta:
Cheesy Chicken and Spinach Pie, 45
Fruity Field Greens Salad with Apricot
Glazed Chicken, 49
Mediterranean Bell Peppers, 91
Mediterranean Eggs Benedict, 31
Mediterranean Stuffed Chicken
with Roasted Vegetables, 47
Spinach and Feta Pork Tenderloin
en Croute, 57

Mozzarella (grated):
Best Crab Dip Ever, 19
Cheesy Chicken and Spinach Pie, 45
Italian Zucchini Gondolas, 95
Mediterranean Eggs Benedict, 31
Mediterranean Stuffed Chicken with
Roasted Vegetables, 47
Mini-Pizzas, 21
Pepperoni Stuffed Chicken, 43
Spinach and Artichoke Eggs Benedict, 35

Parmesan (grated):
Italian Zucchini Gondolas, 95
Spinach and Artichoke Eggs Benedict, 35

Cherry(ies):
Fresh, sweet and dark:
Fruity Field Greens Salad with Apricot
Glazed Chicken, 49
Sweet and Sour Cherry Pork Chops, 65

Chicken:
Breasts:
Angela's Guilt-Free Chicken Salad, 41
Cheesy Chicken and Spinach Pie, 45
Fruity Field Greens Salad with Apricot
Glazed Chicken, 49
Mediterranean Stuffed Chicken with
Roasted Vegetables, 47
Pepperoni Stuffed Chicken, 43
Thai Masaman Chicken, 51

Chipotle Chili Powder:
Angela's Spicy Deviled Eggs, 15
Festive Fruit and Field Greens Salad with Spicy
Chipotle Shrimp, 71
Grilled Zucchini and Red Onion Skewers with
Orange Chipotle Marinade, 76
Southwestern Chimichurri Trout, 79
Spicy Tilapia with Fruit Salsa, 75

Chocolate Hazelnut Spread:
Chocolate Hazelnut Lava Cakes, 103

Chocolate Shavings:
Chocolate Hazelnut Lava Cakes, 103

Cilantro:
Angela's Slow Cooker Ropa Vieja, 89
Citrus Rice Pilaf, 77
Festive Fruit and Field Greens Salad with Spicy
Chipotle Shrimp, 71
Fiesta Black Bean Dip, 17
Hot Black Bean and Corn Salsa, 80
Southwestern Chimichurri Trout, 79
Spicy Tilapia with Fruit Salsa, 75

Cinnamon:
Ceylon:
Amaretto Banana Waffles, 25
Brandied Peaches, 101
Jasmine Rice, 52
Strawberry Shortcake, 109
Thai Masaman Chicken, 51
Thai Noodle Bowl with Shrimp, 73
Korintaje:
Baked Cinnamon and Sugar Amaretto
French Toast, 29

Coconut Milk:
Thai Masaman Chicken, 51
Thai Noodle Bowl with Shrimp, 73

Corn Starch:
Sweet and Sour Cherry Pork Chops, 65

Corn:
Fresh:
Hot Black Bean and Corn Salsa, 80
Sweet Corn Muffins, 59
Pickled Baby:
Thai Noodle Bowl with Shrimp, 73

Cornmeal:
Sweet Corn Muffins, 59

Cream:
Heavy Cream:
Best Crab Dip Ever, 19
Sour Cream:
Best Crab Dip Ever, 19
Fiesta Black Bean Dip, 17
Spinach and Artichoke Eggs Benedict, 35
Spinach and Feta Pork Tenderloin en Croute, 57
Whipped:
Strawberry Shortcake, 109

Cumin:
Fiesta Black Bean Dip, 17

Curry:
Red Curry Paste:
Thai Masaman Chicken, 51
Thai Noodle Bowl with Shrimp, 73

Egg(s):
Amaretto Banana Waffles, 25
Angela's Moist and Buttery Pound Cake, 107
Angela's Spicy Deviled Eggs, 15
Baked Cinnamon and Sugar Amaretto
French Toast, 29
Cheesy Chicken and Spinach Pie, 45
Chocolate Hazelnut Lava Cakes, 103
Cinnamon Raisin Stuffed French Toast Casserole, 27
Italian Zucchini Gondolas, 95

Lemon Poppy Seed Pound Cake, 105
Mediterranean Eggs Benedict, 31
Mediterranean Hollandaise Sauce, 32
Mediterranean Stuffed Bell Peppers, 91
Spinach and Artichoke Eggs Benedict, 35
Spicy Hollandaise Sauce, 36
Spinach and Feta Pork Tenderloin en Croute, 57
Sweet Corn Muffins, 59

Equivalents, 122

Fish:
Tilapia (filet):
Spicy Tilapia with Fruit Salsa, 75
Trout:
Southwestern Chimichurri Trout, 79

Flour:
All purpose:
Amaretto Banana Waffles, 25
Angela's Moist and Buttery Pound Cake, 107
Lemon Poppy Seed Pound Cake, 105
Sweet Corn Muffins, 59

Frozen Mixed Vegetables:
Mom Buck's Pantry Soup, 59

Fruit Juice:
Berry:
Sweet and Sour Cherry Pork Chops, 65
Fruit Punch:
Sweet and Sour Cherry Pork Chops, 65
Orange:
Citrus Rice Pilaf, 77
Festive Fruit and Field Greens Salad
with Spicy Chipotle Shrimp, 71
Grilled Zucchini and Red Onion Skewers
with Orange Chipotle Marinade, 76
Peach:
Peach Glazed Pork Chops, 61
Sweet and Spiced Green Beans, 63

Garlic:
Angela's Slow Cooker Ropa Vieja, 89
Asian Pot Roast with Asparagus and Potatoes, 87
Best Crab Dip Ever, 19
Fiesta Black Bean Dip, 17
Italian Zucchini Gondolas, 95
Mediterranean Bell Peppers, 91
Mediterranean Breakfast Potatoes, 33
Mediterranean Eggs Benedict, 31
Mediterranean Rice Pilaf, 92
Mediterranean Stuffed Chicken
with Roasted Vegetables, 47
Pepperoni Stuffed Chicken, 43
Rosemary and Garlic Breakfast Potatoes, 37
Southwestern Chimichurri Trout, 79
Spinach and Artichoke Eggs Benedict, 35

Garlic Powder:
Festive Fruit and Field Greens Salad with
Spicy Chipotle Shrimp, 71
Garlic Salt:
Angela's Slow Cooker Ropa Vieja, 89

Ginger:
Ground:
Asian Pot Roast with Asparagus
and Potatoes, 87
Jasmine Rice, 52
Thai Masaman Chicken, 51
Thai Noodle Bowl with Shrimp, 73

Glossary, 124-125

Grape(s):
Angela's Guilt-Free Chicken Salad, 41

Greek Seasoning:
Cheesy Chicken and Spinach Pie, 45
Mediterranean Bell Peppers, 91
Mediterranean Breakfast Potatoes, 33
Mediterranean Eggs Benedict, 31
Mediterranean Rice Pilaf, 92

Mediterranean Stuffed Chicken with Roasted
Vegetables, 47
Spinach and Feta Pork Tenderloin en Croute, 57

Green Beans:
Frozen:
Sweet and Spiced Green Beans, 63

Half and Half:
Allspice Mashed Potatoes, 62
Baked Cinnamon and Sugar Amaretto
French Toast, 27
Cinnamon Raisin Stuffed French Toast Casserole, 29

Ham:
Mini-Pizzas, 19
Mom Buck's Pantry Soup, 59

Hazelnut Liquer:
Chocolate Hazelnut Lava Cakes, 103

Healthy Substitutions, 120-121

Honey:
Asian Pot Roast with Asparagus and Potatoes, 87
Brandies Peaches, 101

Hot Sauce:
Best Crab Dip Ever, 19

Jam (Blackberry or any other):
Cinnamon Raisin Stuffed French Toast Casserole, 27

Lemon Extract:
Lemon Poppy Seed Pound Cake, 105

Lemon Juice:
Best Crab Dip Ever, 19
Mediterranean Stuffed Chicken with
Roasted Vegetables, 47

Lemon(s):
Lemon Poppy Seed Pound Cake, 105

Mediterranean Bell Peppers, 91
Mediterranean Rice Pilaf, 92

Margarine:
Allspice Mashed Potatoes, 62

Mayonnaise:
Angela's Guilt-Free Chicken Salad, 41
Angela's Spicy Deviled Eggs, 15
Best Crab Dip Ever, 19
Festive Fruit and Field Greens Salad with
Spicy Chipotle Shrimp, 71
Spinach and Artichoke Eggs Benedict, 35
Spinach and Feta Pork Tenderloin en Croute, 57

Milk:
Amaretto Banana Waffles, 25
Sweet Corn Muffins, 59

Mixed Field Greens:
Festive Fruit and Field Greens Salad with
Spicy Chipotle Shrimp, 71
Fruity Field Greens Salad with Apricot
Glazed Chicken, 49

Mushroom(s):
White Button:
Angela's Easy Beef Stroganoff, 85

Mustard:
Dry:
Festive Fruit and Field Greens Salad with
Spicy Chipotle Shrimp, 71
Prepared:
Festive Fruit and Field Greens Salad with
Spicy Chipotle Shrimp, 71

Noodles:
Egg:
Angela's Easy Beef Stroganoff, 85
Ramen:
Thai Noodle Bowl with Shrimp, 73

Nuts:
Cashews:
Fruity Field Greens Salad with Apricot
Glazed Chicken, 49
Thai Masaman Chicken, 51

Oil:
Extra Virgin Olive:
Angela's Slow Cooker Ropa Vieja, 89
Bruschetta Pasta, 96
Festive Fruit and Field Greens Salad with
Spicy Chipotle Shrimp, 71
Fruity Field Greens Salad with Apricot
Glazed Chicken, 49
Italian Zucchini Gondolas, 95
Mediterranean Breakfast Potatoes, 33
Mediterranean Eggs Benedict, 31
Mediterranean Stuffed Chicken with
Roasted Vegetables, 47
Peach Glazed Pork Chops, 61
Rosemary and Garlic Breakfast Potatoes, 37
Southwestern Chimichurri Trout, 79
Sweet and Sour Cherry Pork Chops, 65

Olive(s):
Black:
Mediterranean Stuffed Chicken with
Roasted Vegetables, 47
Mini-Pizzas, 21
Pepperoni Stuffed Chicken, 43

Onion(s):
Powder:
Best Crab Dip Ever, 19
Red:
Bruschetta Pasta, 96
Festive Fruit and Field Greens Salad with
Spicy Chipotle Shrimp, 71
Fiesta Black Bean Dip, 17
Grilled Zucchini and Red Onion Skewers
with Orange Chipotle Marinade, 76

Spicy Tilapia with Fruit Salsa, 75
Thai Noodle Bowl with Shrimp, 73
White:
Angela's Slow Cooker Ropa Vieja, 89
Mediterranean Eggs Benedict, 31
Mediterranean Stuffed Chicken with
Roasted Vegetables, 47
Mini-Pizzas, 21
Pepperoni Stuffed Chicken, 43
Yellow:
Angela's Easy Beef Stroganoff, 85
Asian Pot Roast with Asparagus
and Potatoes, 87
Best Crab Dip Ever, 19
Cheesy Chicken and Spinach Pie, 45
Citrus Rice Pilaf, 77
Italian Zucchini Gondolas, 93
Mediterranean Breakfast Potatoes, 33
Rosemary and Garlic Breakfast Potatoes, 37
Thai Masaman Chicken, 51

Orange(s):
Citrus Rice Pilaf, 75
Festive Fruit and Field Greens Salad with
Spicy Chipotle Shrimp, 71
Spicy Tilapia with Fruit Salsa, 75

Oregano:
Dried:
Bruschetta Pasta, 96
Italian Zucchini Gondolas, 95
Pepperoni Stuffed Chicken, 43

Parsley:
Best Crab Dip Ever, 19

Pasta:
Pastina:
Mom Buck's Pantry Soup, 59
Spaghetti:
Bruschetta Pasta, 96
Pepperoni Stuffed Chicken, 43

Pastry Dough:
Spinach and Feta Pork Tenderloin en Croute, 57

Peach(es):
Canned:
Brandied Peaches, 101
Peach Glazed Pork Chops, 61

Pepperoni:
Mini-Pizzas, 21
Pepperoni Stuffed Chicken, 43

Pie Crust:
Cheesy Chicken and Spinach Pie, 45

Pineapple:
Mini-Pizzas, 21

Pizza Sauce:
Mini-Pizzas, 21

Poppy Seeds:
Festive Fruit and Field Greens Salad with
Spicy Chipotle Shrimp, 71
Lemon Poppy Seed Pound Cake, 105

Pork:
Chops:
Peach Glazed Pork Chops, 61
Sweet and Sour Cherry Pork Chops, 65
Ground:
Italian Zucchini Gondolas, 95
Tenderloin:
Spinach and Feta Pork Tenderloin en Croute, 57

Potato(es):
Idaho:
Asian Pot Roast with Asparagus and Potatoes,
87
Red Skinned:
Allspice Mashed Potatoes, 62
Mediterranean Breakfast Potatoes, 33
Rosemary and Garlic Breakfast Potatoes, 37

Preserves:
  Apricot:
    Fruity Field Greens Salad with Apricot Glazed Chicken, 49

Pumpkin Pie Spice:
  Peach Glazed Pork Chops, 61
  Sweet and Spiced Green Beans, 63

Rice:
  Jasmine Rice, 52
  Long Grain:
    Citrus Rice Pilaf, 77
    Mediterranean Rice Pilaf, 92
    Mom Buck's Pantry Soup, 59

Rosemary:
  Dried:
    Rosemary and Garlic Breakfast Potatoes, 37

Seafood:
  Crab (or imitation):
    Best Crab Dip Ever, 19
  Shrimp:
    Festive Fruit and Field Greens Salad with Spicy Chipotle Shrimp, 71
    Thai Noodle Bowl with Shrimp, 73

Serrano Chiles:
  Fiesta Black Bean Dip, 17

Semi-Sweet Chocolate Baking Squares:
  Chocolate Hazelnut Lava Cakes, 101

Soup:
  Can Cream of Chicken Soup:
    Angela's Easy Beef Stroganoff, 85
  Can Cream of Mushroom Soup:
    Angela's Easy Beef Stroganoff, 85

Soy Sauce:
  Asian Pot Roast with Asparagus and Potatoes, 85

Spinach:
  Fresh:
    Thai Noodle Bowl with Shrimp, 73
  Frozen and Chopped:
    Cheesy Chicken and Spinach Pie, 45
    Mediterranean Eggs Benedict, 31
    Mediterranean Stuffed Chicken with Roasted Vegetables, 47
    Spinach and Artichoke Eggs Benedict, 33
    Spinach and Feta Pork Tenderloin en Croute, 57

Strawberry(ies):
  Festive Fruit and Field Greens Salad with Spicy Chipotle Shrimp, 71
  Spicy Tilapia with Fruit Salsa, 75
  Strawberry Shortcake, 109

Sugar:
  Granulated:
    Amaretto Banana Waffles, 25
    Angela's Moist and Buttery Pound Cake, 107
    Baked Cinnamon and Sugar Amaretto French Toast, 29
    Chocolate Hazelnut Lava Cakes, 103
    Fruity Field Greens Salad with Apricot Glazed Chicken, 49
    Lemon Poppy Seed Pound Cake, 105
    Strawberry Shortcake, 107
    Sweet Corn Muffins, 59

Sweet Relish:
  Angela's Spicy Deviled Eggs, 13

Syrup:
  Corn:
    Sweet Corn Muffins, 57
  Maple:
    Amaretto Banana Waffles, 25
    Baked Cinnamon and Sugar Amaretto French Toast, 29
    Cinnamon Raisin Stuffed French Toast Casserole, 27

Thyme:
  Dried:
    Bruschetta Pasta, 96
    Italian Zucchini Gondolas, 95
    Pepperoni Stuffed Chicken, 43

Tomato(es):
  Chopped (canned):
    Bruschetta Pasta, 96
  Crushed:
    Mediterranean Bell Peppers, 91
    Mediterranean Rice Pilaf, 92
    Mom Buck's Pantry Soup, 59
    Pepperoni Stuffed Chicken, 43
  Fresh:
    Angela's Guilt Free Chicken Salad, 41
    Fiesta Black Bean Dip, 17
    Mediterranean Eggs Benedict, 31
  Mild Green Chiles (canned):
    Angela's Slow Cooker Ropa Vieja, 89
    Hot Black Bean and Corn Salsa, 80
  Paste:
    Angela's Slow Cooker Ropa Vieja, 89
    Pepperoni Stuffed Chicken, 43
  Roma:
    Cheesy Chicken and Spinach Pie, 45
  Sauce:
    Bruschetta Pasta, 96
    Italian Zucchini Gondolas, 95
    Pepperoni Stuffed Chicken, 41

Tortilla Chips:
  Festive Fruit and Field Greens Salad with
  Spicy Chipotle Shrimp, 71
  Fiesta Black Bean Dip, 17

Vanilla Ice Cream:
  Chocolate Hazelnut Lava Cakes, 103

Vanilla:
  Angela's Moist and Buttery Pound Cake, 105
  Cinnamon Raisin Stuffed French Toast Casserole, 25
  Lemon Poppy Seed Pound Cake, 103

Vinegar:
  Balsamic:
    Bruschetta Pasta, 96
  Red Wine:
    Angela's Slow Cooker Ropa Vieja, 89
    Mediterranean Bell Peppers, 91
    Mediterranean Rice Pilaf, 92
    Sweet and Sour Cherry Pork Chops, 65
  Rice Wine:
    Asian Pot Roast with Asparagus
    and Potatoes, 87
    Fruity Field Greens Salad with Apricot
    Glazed Chicken, 49

Worcestershire Sauce:
  Best Crab Dip Ever, 19
  Fruity Field Greens Salad with Apricot
  Glazed Chicken, 49

Yogurt:
  Plain:
    Angela's Easy Beef Stroganoff, 85
    Angela's Guilt-Free Chicken Salad, 41
    Angela's Moist and Buttery Pound Cake, 107
    Lemon Poppy Seed Pound Cake, 105

Zucchini:
  Grilled Zucchini and Red Onion Skewers with
  Orange Chipotle Marinade, 74
  Italian Zucchini Gondolas, 95

Angela's Not-So-Fable About the Table

6

My niece and nephew are so much fun! Over the years we have played together at the park, played "airplane" where I "fly" them around in the air and have played various games that children under the age of 2 can play. As they have gotten older, their level of interaction with us and their ability to participate in more complex activities has really become noticeable.

A couple of years back, circumstances took my husband and me to Florida. It was seven hours from home and we sure missed the family. We knew that we were missing out on my niece and nephew growing up and just random get togethers with everyone, but we couldn't leave Florida right away. As you can imagine, it became our top priority to move back home just as soon as we could!

When we came back, it was a year later and my niece and nephew were conveniently a year older. They were now ages 4 and 2. Before we moved, they had been a lot of fun to be with, but now they were both old enough to be able to enjoy our company, remember who we were and ask when we would be able to visit again. It was so great to be home!

I began to think about more fun activities that we could do together now that they were a bit older. I would go to local craft stores and pick up fun crafts to do with them. Local book stores had kits for making balloon animals and that was a lot of fun for an entire afternoon! The swan hat that I made for my niece to wear on her head was a hit while my nephew would let air out of the balloons and watch them race through the air like colorful jets!

Then, it suddenly dawned on me. Why on Earth had I not opted to cook with them yet? Cooking was my passion. Mom Buck's visits had been the highlight of my week for 18 years and because of her, I didn't see it as a chore, but rather a great way to de-stress and be creative! I could inspire them the way Mom Buck had inspired me!

A few months after creating my cooking show, 'Kick Back and Kook!' I invited the children over to cook with me. I figured it would be a great idea to film it so that years down the road we would be able to watch it and enjoy it all over again. We all pretended to be celebrity chefs and had a GREAT time! We made mini-pizzas (found in the 'munchie' section of this cookbook), they had a blast and they just hammed it up for the camera!

After we finished everything, I asked their mom and dad if they minded if I uploaded their video to my website because it turned out so well. They had been too entertaining not to at least consider it! They said it was no problem and later, my niece and nephew saw it on the computer and just knew that they had become movie stars! Plus, now they ask when they can come over and cook again! But that wasn't all!

I can't even begin to tell you how many countless emails I received from parents telling me that they had assumed that their children were too young to cook; they didn't know of any recipes to prepare; and the recipe we demonstrated was a great idea that they were eager to try. It was so inspiring and it felt really good to make a difference to my niece, nephew and all of the parents watching at home. 'Kooking with Kids' has become a regular activity for me, my niece and my nephew! We enjoy the bond we've created through cooking and they LOVE learning how to cook!

MORAL OF THE STORY:

Patience and positive reinforcement in the kitchen can create a lifetime of fun and value for the children in your life. Get them involved, even if it's just stirring something or adding a simple ingredient like grated cheese. Even better, who knows who you could inspire just by people knowing that you inspired them!

Healthy Substitutions ....

Looking to eat a bit healthier? Consider these substitutions

Broth?
Make broth with bouillon cubes. There will be no fat, but keep in mind that they **can be high in sodium**. Look for broth (in a box or canned) that is 99% fat free AND low sodium if you need both.

Butter vs. Margarine?
Margarine is typically better for you than butter because margarine is made with vegetable oil which contains no cholesterol. However, margarine is often processed by a method called "hydrogenation" which creates an unhealthy ingredient called "hydrogenated oil". Look for cholesterol free margarine that has NO hydrogenated oil and no transfats.
If you see hydrogenated oil in the ingredients of the margarine, it is no better than butter because hydrogenated oil is similar to animal fat, which is used to create butter and does contain cholesterol.

Buttermilk?
In baking, substitute fat-free or low-fat sour cream OR fat-free/low-fat yogurt. The results produce the same, moist goodness in muffins, fruit breads, pound cakes, cakes and cupcakes.

Cheese?
Look for low-fat, not fat free. Fat free doesn't melt properly, but low-fat does and still tastes really good!

Cream cheese?
Low-fat and fat-free really do taste the same. Go for lower fat every time!

Eggs?
So, you want to splurge on those French Toast recipes, but think you can't? Think again! Consider using a healthy egg substitute. The carton will tell you which measurement equals 1 egg. Use the carton instructions for the same number of eggs and continue to follow the recipe as directed! Sorry! Eggs Benedict is just decadent. Maybe you'll just make that one for special occasions!

Half and half?
Guess what! There actually **IS** a fat free half and half! If you can't find it, you can always substitute soy with added calcium or a lower fat milk. Just remember, soy is metabolized within the body as estrogen, so check with your doctor before switching to soy.

Milk?
Even when drinking 1%, there's still quite a bit of fat in milk, particularly if you drink a lot of it. It has been scientifically proven that adults benefit very little from the consumption of milk. Consider a low-fat or fat-free yogurt over your crispy cereal instead of milk. Soy Milk can also be an alternative. Again, women need to be aware that Soy Milk

is metabolized within the body to estrogen. Ask your doctor about whether or not soy products are a good alternative for you! If your doctor says ok, consider substituting it in place of milk or half and half in your recipes!

Oil?

In baking, substitute applesauce for your oil! Your end result will be moister and MUCH less fattening. Take half of the measurement of oil and substitute that amount of applesauce (ie: 1 c. oil = ½ cup applesauce).When sautéing or searing with oil, heat your pan before you add the oil. You can sometimes reduce your oil by 1 T. because the heat causes the oil to cover more area of the pan. Extra virgin olive oil is the best oil you can use for cooking, just not for frying. It raises "good" cholesterol and helps control the "bad." It is also contains natural antioxidants. When at all possible, use it! I rarely ever use vegetable oil any more.

Pizza?

Don't give it up! Consider using whole wheat English muffins in place of biscuits or a whole wheat pizza crust. Use turkey or veggie pepperoni and low-fat mozzarella cheese. Trust me, it's still VERY tasty!

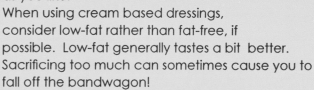

Salad Dressing?

Why bother adding the oil? Just use apple cider vinegar, rice wine vinegar, balsamic vinegar, red wine vinegar, lemon or lime juice. It's fat-free, so use as much as you like!
When using cream based dressings, consider low-fat rather than fat-free, if possible. Low-fat generally tastes a bit better. Sacrificing too much can sometimes cause you to fall off the bandwagon!
Also, have 2 T. of dressing in a small cup on the side. Dip your fork in the dressing and then dive into your salad. Because the dressing is concentrated in one place, it will taste like more when it's actually less!

Sour Cream?

In baking, you can substitute low-fat or fat free without it altering the taste or texture of what you are making. Low fat can taste just as good as the regular on baked potatoes or consider using low-fat cottage cheese.

Easy Measuring Equivalents ......

1 tablespoon (T. or tbsp) = 3 teaspoons (tsp)

1/16 cup (c.) = 1 tablespoon

1/8 cup = 2 tablespoons

1/6 cup = 2 tablespoons + 2 teaspoons

1/4 cup = 4 tablespoons

1/3 cup = 5 tablespoons + 1 teaspoon

3/8 cup = 6 tablespoons

1/2 cup = 8 tablespoons

2/3 cup = 10 tablespoons + 2 teaspoons

3/4 cup = 12 tablespoons

1 cup = 48 teaspoons, 16 tablespoons or 8 oz.

1 pint (pt) = 2 cups

1 quart (qt) = 4 cups or 2 pints

1 gallon (gal) = 16 cups or 4 quarts

16 ounces (oz) = 1 pound (lb)

When you go shopping, try to remember how many ounces equal a cup, 1/2 cup, etc. If you know that your recipe only calls for a cup of something and you are certain that you'll only use it once, buy 8 ounces of it and there will be no waste because 8 ounces = 1 cup! I frequently use this information for things like yogurt, sour cream and heavy cream.

Tips for Grocery Shopping..............

Dislike long trips to the grocery store? I think most people do. What I have learned over the years is that there are basic ingredients that I consistently use over and over again. These ingredients that I use frequently can be used in many different combinations, so I don't have to worry about eating the same thing repeatedly. So, what I do to simplify things is I replace these basic items as soon as I run out. Sound like a chore? I promise - not really! Make the one big trip for all of these items and you'll be well on your way to light shopping from now on!

Most stores that I shop at for items such as wrapping paper, gifts for nieces/nephews, bridal showers and baby showers also have a grocery section. I find that if I keep a running list of the basic items that I need, invariably I have to pick up a gift for someone, so while I'm out shopping for something else, I will just pick up the 3 – 5 items that I have just run out of. Simple, right? I think so!

Here is a list of things that will simplify your life if you keep them in stock at all times:

• Boneless, skinless chicken breasts **(frozen if not used right away)**
• Boneless pork chops **(frozen if not used right away)**
• Ground beef **(frozen if not used right away)**
• 1 dozen grade A large eggs **(all of my recipes require this size egg)**
• 4 sticks of butter/ margarine
• Minced garlic **(keeps longer if you buy it in a jar, already minced)**
• Lemon juice **(or fresh lemons if you go through them quickly)**
• Dried basil
• Dried oregano
• Greek Seasoning
• Dried bread crumbs **(plain, you can always add your own seasoning)**
• Cream cheese
• Frozen, chopped spinach
• Crushed tomatoes
• At least 2 cans of tomato paste
• 1 large can of tomato sauce
• 2 cans of black beans
• 2 cans of tomatoes with
• Mild chiles
• Red wine vinegar
• Apple cider vinegar
• White distilled vinegar **(for home remedies and ease of peeling boiled eggs!)**
• 2 cans of beef broth
• 2 cans of chicken broth
• 2 cans of cream of chicken or cream of mushroom soup **(can be used interchangeably)**
• 1 – 2 c. bag of grated mozzarella cheese
• 1 – 1 c. bag of parmesan cheese **(or perhaps they come in 1 ¼ c. bags)**
• All-purpose flour
• Cornmeal
• Rice
• Egg noodles/spaghetti/ small pasta
• Granulated sugar
• Cornstarch
• Baking powder **(if you plan to make waffles or cakes often – it will lose it's rising power after a certain period of time,** so only buy it when you need it if it will be used only every 6 months)
• Baking soda
• Cinnamon
• Baking chocolate

Ok. The baking chocolate may not be a necessity in your home, but it is in mine! Ha!! This may seem like a long list, but trust me, you will use these items so frequently that you may just be surprised at how convenient it is to have all of these items in your pantry! Hopefully, the only trips you should ever have to make to the store are for perishable items that you may not use quickly enough to store them (ie: herbs, fresh produce, etc).

Happy shopping!

Glossary of Ingredients

Apple Cider Vinegar: A pale, golden vinegar with the fruity flavor and crisp tang of apple cider.

Balsamic Vinegar: Made from reduced grape juice and is aged and blended for many years in a succession of casks made of different woods and gradually diminishing in size. The result is a thick, tart-sweet, intensely aromatic vinegar. Great on salads in place of dressing.

Basil (dried): An intensely aromatic green-leaved herb popular in Italian and French cooking. Its sweet and somewhat spicy flavor enhances tomato-based dishes and sauces, and Italian pesto. In my opinion, you can never use too much of it!

Cardamom: is a sweet, exotic-tasting spice. The small, round seeds grow inside husk-like pods and can be bought ground. If you buy them whole, you can grind them yourself in a mortar and pestle, a coffee grinder or spice grinder.

Challah: A rich, slightly sweet yeast bread that includes eggs. The dough is divided into three long strands and braided before it is baked. Typically found in the bakery section of your grocery store, made by the bakers in the store or at traditional bakeries.

Chipotle Chile Powder: Made from ripened jalapeño chiles that are smoke-dried. Has a smoky, spicy flavor that brings a lot of depth to your recipes, but be careful not to use too much or the smoky flavor will be overpowered by the heat of the chiles!

Cilantro: A leafy, green herb resembling flat-leaf (Italian) parsley, so be sure you have the right one! It has a sharp, aromatic, somewhat astringent flavor. Popular in Latin American and Asian cuisines, it is commonly referred to as Chinese parsley or fresh coriander. Store cilantro in the refrigerator, wrapped in paper towels and enclosed in a plastic bag. Fresh is better than dried.

Ceylon Cinnamon: Complex and fragrant with a citrus overtone which makes it distinctly different from that found in traditional grocery stores. Ceylon Cinnamon is best when added to desserts that are made with fruit (apple pie, peach cobbler, glazed pears, etc.).

Coconut Milk: A rich, creamy liquid made from water and coconut pulp. A staple ingredient in Thai curries and other Asian dishes throughout Southeast Asia. Unsweetened coconut milk is available in cans at well-stocked grocery stores on the ethnic foods aisle and in Asian markets. Do not substitute cream of coconut because it will be too thick and alter the flavor.

Crushed Tomatoes: A canned tomato product that consists of finely chopped tomatoes combined with tomato purée and sometimes flavored with herbs. Unless you know what you are going to be using them for, it is best to get them without herbs, ie: Italian flavors and Greek flavors are much different, but both can call for crushed tomatoes.

Extra Virgin Olive Oil: Commonly referred to as one of the healing fats, it is one of the healthiest oils to cook with. Store in a dark, cool place.

Galangal: Related to and resembles ginger, but has a mildly mustard-like, slightly medicinal taste; ginger is not an acceptable substitute. When used in combination with other spices for Asian dishes, it is a great accompaniment for depth of flavor with no medicinal taste at all. Found in red curry paste, but not used by itself in any of my recipes.

Garlic Powder: Made from dehydrated garlic flakes that have been ground into a powdery substance. It is used as a seasoning. If you don't buy a high quality garlic powder, then you may have to use a lot of it if you plan to substitute it for fresh. It will do in a pinch, but fresh garlic is generally a better choice unless you are searing it into pork, chicken or steak for flavor (high heat can cause fresh garlic to take on a bitter flavor, therefore; making it a poor candidate for searing into meats).

Garlic Salt: A combination of garlic powder and salt. When using this in place of garlic powder, be VERY careful and use sparingly or you'll have a dish that is too salty to eat!

Ginger: Yields a strong-flavored spice. May be purchased fresh and easiest peeled with a spoon, surprisingly! Has a lively, hot flavor and peppery aroma. Select fresh ginger that is firm, not shriveled. Wrap in a paper towel and refrigerate for 2 to 3 weeks. Ground, dried ginger, which is more subtle and sweet in flavor, is sold in jars or tins; store in a cool, dark place for up to 6 months.

Greek Seasoning: A combination of dried lemon peel, garlic, oregano, black pepper and marjoram. Everything you need in one bottle of seasoning or combine the above listed ingredients in the proportions that you like best.

Half and Half: A commercial dairy product that consists of half milk and half light cream. Not to be confused with whipping cream or heavy cream. When a recipe calls for half and half, you can usually substitute whipping cream. However, do not consider substituting half and half when a recipe calls for whipping cream or heavy cream.

Heavy Cream: Also called whipping cream, has a milk fat content of between 36 to 40 percent. When whipped, it will double in volume. Half and half will not double in volume, so substituting half and half when you do not have heavy cream will not usually work.

Korintje Cinnamon: Sweet and mellow, it is reminiscent of freshly baked sweet breads, cinnamon rolls and cookies. Best served in bread dishes, pie crusts, waffles, pancakes or over oatmeal.

Lemon Grass: is a stiff, reed-like grass with a sharp, lemony flavor. It contributes an aromatic, citrus-like flavor to Southeast Asian recipes and is found in red curry paste, but not actually used by itself in any of these recipes.

Marjoram: A pungent, aromatic herb used fresh or dried to season meats (particularly lamb), poultry, seafood, vegetables, and eggs. Has a bit of a licorice flavor to it, in my opinion.

Onions:

Green: Tiny white onions with long green stems, generally found in the produce section near fresh herbs. Both the green leaves and white bulbs can be used raw or cooked for their mild but still pronounced onion flavor. Also called scallions or spring onions.

Red: Also called Spanish onions, are medium to large onions that have purplish red skins and red-tinged white flesh with a mild, sweet flavor. Great for cooking, but also ideal for sandwiches, salads and burgers because of their sweet flavor and attractive presentation.

White: Have both white skin and white flesh; tend to be sweet and mild in flavor. If they are unavailable, substitute with mild yellow onions.

Yellow: are the common, white-fleshed, large onions distinguished by their strong flavor and dry, yellowish brown skin.

Onion powder: Made from ground dehydrated onions. It is used as a seasoning. Typically good in sauces when combined with other flavors, but not a good substitute for real onions. I often puree onions and add to a sauce when someone tells me that they like onion flavor, but not the texture of onions.

Oregano: Also known as wild marjoram, this is an aromatic, spicy Mediterranean herb sold as fresh sprigs or chopped dried leaves. This popular herb is used to season all types of savory dishes, especially tomato-based recipes.

Red Curry Paste: A classic Thai blend of red chiles, garlic, onions, lemongrass, cilantro, and galangal. It is sold in Asian markets or on the ethnic aisle of your grocery store, usually in a small jar. A little bit goes a long way, so use sparingly!

Rice Wine Vinegar: Also called rice vinegar. Usually found on ethnic foods aisle, not vinegar aisle, but check both. Chinese rice vinegars are milder and less acidic than regular vinegar. There are three basic types - black, red and white -as well as sweetened black vinegars. The black variety is somewhat similar to balsamic vinegar, while red vinegar has both a sweet and tart taste. White vinegar is the closest in acidity and flavor to regular vinegar. There are no hard and fast rules, but black vinegar is generally recommended for braised dishes and as a dipping sauce, red vinegar for soups, noodle and seafood dishes, and white for sweet and sour dishes and for pickling.

Serrano Chiles: are small and slender-up to 2 inches long and about 1/2 inch wide. These fresh green or red chiles are about as spicy as jalapeños, which are notably sharper and very hot. Removing the seeds will cut down on the heat as the seeds are the source of the majority of their heat.

Tomato Paste: A concentrate of puréed tomatoes commonly sold in small cans and used to add flavor and body to sauces. For superior flavor, look for tubes of imported double-strength tomato concentrate in Italian delicatessens and well-stocked food stores, but keep in mind that these will cost more. Tomato paste is also commonly used to thicken sauces.

Tomato Sauce: A consists of tomato purée enhanced with various flavorings, including onions, garlic, spices, or herbs.

Whipping Cream: Also called heavy cream, has a milk fat content of between 36 to 40 percent. When whipped, it will double in volume. Half and half will not double in volume, so substituting half and half when you do not have heavy cream will not usually work.

"You did it!
THANK *YOU* for letting me help!"

Angela

www.kickbackkook.com